AGENTIC AI SYSTEMS

Architectures and Design Patterns for Autonomous Intelligence

Oliver Tomlinson

TABLE OF CONTENTS

INTRODUCTION

I almost called this book something else. For a while the working title was "Stop Chaining Prompts," which tells you more about my frustration than the actual content. I had spent the better part of two years watching smart developers build fragile systems, and the problem was rarely incompetence. It was that nobody had told them they were solving the wrong problem. They were tuning prompts when they needed to rethink the architecture entirely.

This book is a response to that. It is for the developer who has gotten reasonably good at prompt engineering and is still watching the system break in embarrassing ways at two in the morning. It is for the product lead who keeps hearing "we need to add AI" and is not sure what that means beyond wrapping a GPT call in an API endpoint. And it is for the curious person who reads about autonomous AI agents in the news and wants to understand what is real versus what is marketing.

Before we go any further, I want to be clear about what kind of book this is. There are already plenty of books that explain what large language models are, how transformers work mathematically, and why attention mechanisms are theoretically elegant. Those books have value. This is not one of them. This book is about building systems that run, that do work, that fail in understandable ways and recover from those failures without someone watching over them. Everything here is grounded in what actually works when you deploy it, not in what looks good in a paper or a conference presentation.

What Agentic AI Actually Means

The simplest version goes like this. A regular language model takes your input, processes it, and gives you back output. One shot, done. An agent does something qualitatively different: it has a goal, it takes steps toward that goal, it uses tools, and it adjusts based on what happens. The conversation is not the product. The task completion is.

GPT-4 can write a fantastic email. An agent can figure out who to send it to, draft it, check the calendar for follow-up timing, send it when you are most likely to get a response, and flag you if nobody replies after a week. The underlying model is the same. The architecture around it is completely different.

That gap between "I have access to a capable language model" and "I have built something that runs autonomously and does useful work" is what this book tries to close.

I should be upfront about what this book is not. It does not cover reinforcement learning in depth, or the theoretical foundations of decision theory, or most of what academic researchers mean when they say "agents." I am a practitioner and this is a practitioner's book. We will use LangGraph, CrewAI, AutoGen: frameworks that exist today, that you can install today, that real companies are shipping to production. The research literature is valuable, but it is not where most of the practical knowledge about building these systems lives.

The other thing this book is not is a hype vehicle. The AI space has no shortage of people telling you that autonomous agents will replace entire job categories within eighteen months, that every workflow will be automated by next year, that we are weeks away from systems that can do everything. I find this kind of writing actively unhelpful, because it sets expectations that production deployments then fail to meet, which makes teams lose confidence in tools that would have worked fine if applied more carefully. What I have tried to do instead is describe what these systems actually do well, what they genuinely struggle with, and how to design around the struggles rather than pretend they do not exist.

Why I Wrote This

The moment that changed my thinking happened during a demo I was giving to a product team. I had built what I thought was a sophisticated system: a multi-step research assistant that could pull sources, summarize them, and draft a report. The product manager asked a simple question. "What happens if one of the sources times out?"

I did not have a good answer. The system would fail, silently, and produce a report with gaps it did not flag.

That question nagged at me for weeks. I realized I had been thinking about AI systems the same way I thought about a single API call. You send a request, you get a response. But a real autonomous system is something that runs over time, encounters unexpected situations, and needs to make decisions when things do not go as planned. I had a language model. I did not have an agent.

The architecture I eventually built to fix that problem had a coordinator that tracks state, workers that handle specific subtasks, and a delegator that decides when to retry versus when to escalate. That structure ended up being the core pattern this book is built around. It is one pattern among several, but it is the one I kept returning to because it makes the failure modes explicit and manageable.

Getting stuck on YAML syntax is still a regular occurrence for me, if that helps. I am not presenting this as solved problems from a comfortable distance. The field is genuinely hard, the tooling is immature in places, and things that worked six months ago sometimes need to be rebuilt because a framework released a breaking update. I have tried to write the book I wish had existed when I was starting.

There is also something worth saying about the pace of change in this field specifically. Between the time I started writing this book and the time I finished it, three major framework versions shipped with breaking changes, two new model families were released that changed what was practical to build, and at least two startups I had been following as examples of good agentic architecture either pivoted or shut down. I have tried to focus on the underlying principles and patterns that survive these changes rather than on specific API signatures that will likely look different in six months. But I want to be honest that staying current in this space requires ongoing attention, not just reading one book.

A New Kind of Intelligence

When people hear "agentic AI" for the first time, they often think of science fiction: fully autonomous robots, systems that make decisions entirely on their own, artificial general intelligence in a box. The reality is both more modest and more interesting than that. What we actually have are systems that can pursue goals over time, use software tools to take actions, remember things across interactions, and adapt their approach based on what happens. They are not conscious, they are not infallible, and they are not going to replace human judgment for anything that actually matters. But they can do a remarkable amount of useful work within a well-defined scope, and the scope of what counts as well-defined has been expanding rapidly.

The best mental model I have found is to think of an agentic system as a very capable junior employee who works incredibly fast but needs clear instructions, good documentation, and human oversight for anything with significant consequences. This employee can do research, draft documents, execute routine workflows, monitor systems, and coordinate between multiple tasks simultaneously. They will sometimes make mistakes, especially in situations they have not encountered before. They need to be able to ask for help when they are uncertain. And they need a clear understanding of what they are authorized to do on their own versus what requires approval.

That framing shapes everything about how I approach system design in this book. The goal is not to build something that operates completely without human involvement. The goal is to build something that handles the routine cases autonomously while escalating the non-routine cases gracefully. That distinction sounds simple but getting it right in practice is the core challenge of agentic system design.

Who This Book Is For

The primary audience is developers who are already comfortable with Python, have worked with at least one large language model API, and are ready to move beyond single-call applications. You do not need to have built an agentic system before. You do need to be willing to think about software architecture, not just prompt engineering.

Product managers and technical leads will also find this useful, particularly the sections on governance, evaluation, and human-in-the-loop design. Understanding what these systems can and cannot do, and what it takes to operate them responsibly, is increasingly important for anyone making decisions about where AI fits into a product or workflow.

I have written assuming you have basic familiarity with Python and REST APIs. I have not assumed familiarity with any specific AI framework, since we will cover LangGraph, CrewAI, and AutoGen from the ground up as they become relevant.

What Is in Here

The book moves from foundations to implementation in a fairly linear way, though each section can stand on its own if you are coming with specific questions.

Section I covers what an agent actually is: the difference between a language model and a goal-directed system, how memory and planning work, where the various generative model architectures fit in, and why the transformer became the engine powering all of this. If you are already solid on these concepts, you can skim this section and use it as a reference.

Section II gets into architecture. Reactive versus deliberative agents, how to compose them into hybrid systems, the coordinator-worker-delegator pattern, how tool use works in practice, and the underappreciated problem of memory and state management. This is the heart of the book for people who are actively building.

Section III is about scale and operations. Multi-agent systems, evaluation, human oversight, and governance. This is where things get genuinely hard and where the most production failures happen. I have tried to be honest about the difficulty here rather than glossing over it.

Section IV closes with applied examples, case studies, and design canvases you can adapt to your domain. These are drawn from real deployments, and I have included the failure modes and lessons learned, not just the success stories.

On the code: there is quite a bit of it, but I have tried to keep examples concrete and runnable rather than illustrative pseudocode. The examples use Python because that is where the ecosystem is most developed. The architectural ideas transfer to other languages and frameworks.

One honest caveat before we start. The field moves fast enough that some of what I have written will be outdated by the time you read it. That is unavoidable. What I have tried to do is ground the book in principles that will stay true even as the tooling evolves. The reasons why you need memory, why planning matters, why human oversight is not optional: those hold regardless of which framework is newest. The specific code you will probably need to adapt.

I hope the book is useful. Build something real with it.

SECTION I: Foundations of Agentic Intelligence

Chapter 1

From Language Models to Goal-Driven Systems

The easiest way I have found to explain the difference between a language model and an agent is this: a language model is a very sophisticated autocomplete. An agent is something that is trying to accomplish something.

That sounds like a small distinction until you actually sit down and try to build one.

GPT-4, Claude, Gemini: these models are genuinely impressive at generating plausible next tokens given a context. When that context is well-formed and the task is one the model has seen variations of during training, the output can be remarkably good. The problem is that generating plausible text and accomplishing a goal reliably over multiple steps with real-world tools and unpredictable conditions are two very different things. The gap between them is mostly architectural rather than a matter of making the model bigger or smarter.

I want to be specific about what I mean by "architectural," because this distinction matters for everything that follows. When I say the problem is architectural, I mean that you cannot solve it by switching to a better model, writing a more carefully crafted prompt, or adding more examples to your context. The problem is structural: a language model, by itself, lacks certain capabilities that are necessary for autonomous operation. No amount of prompting adds those capabilities. You have to engineer them into the system around the model.

Why Language Models Alone Are Not Enough

Consider what happens when you use ChatGPT to help with a research task. You paste in a question, it gives you an answer, you refine the question, it gives you a better answer. There is a person in the loop doing all the work of deciding what to ask next, evaluating whether the output is useful, figuring out what additional information is needed. The model is a capable text processor. The intelligence about what to do next is still entirely yours.

Now imagine you want to automate that loop. You want a system that can take a research question, figure out what sources to consult, retrieve them, extract the relevant parts, synthesize them, and give you a finished report without you having to drive every step. This is where language models alone start to show their structural limits.

The core issue is state. A language model does not remember what it just did. Every call to the model is stateless: it receives tokens, predicts tokens, and the interaction ends there. If you want the model to know that it already tried a search query and got poor results, or that it is on step three of a five-step plan, you have to engineer that tracking yourself. The model does not maintain awareness of its own progress; you have to maintain it on the model's behalf.

This is more consequential than it might seem. Consider a research task that requires gathering information from eight different sources, synthesizing those sources into a coherent summary, checking the summary for factual consistency, and formatting the output according to a specific template. A human researcher doing this task maintains a mental model of where they are in the process: which sources they have looked at, what they have already synthesized, what still needs checking. A language model has none of this. Each call starts fresh. The model has no awareness of what it has already done unless you explicitly encode that information in the prompt for each call.

The second issue is tools. Language models generate text. They do not actually search the web, or query a database, or send an API request, unless you build infrastructure around them that intercepts what they generate and executes it. The model can describe what it would do. Getting it to actually do it requires a wrapper that can parse its output and translate it into real actions. This wrapper is non-trivial to build correctly, especially for tools that have side effects, return complex data structures, or fail in ways that need to be handled gracefully.

The third issue is error handling. Real-world tasks fail in ways that a stateless model has no concept of. An API times out. A web page returns a 403. A search query returns irrelevant results. A language model, confronted with unexpected input, will typically try to generate something plausible rather than recognize that something has gone wrong and adapt accordingly. You need logic outside the model to catch failures and decide what to do next: retry the same approach, try a different approach, or escalate to a human.

The fourth issue, which gets less attention than it deserves, is evaluation. A language model generating a response has no mechanism for checking whether the response is actually good. It does not ask itself whether the answer makes sense, whether it has covered all the required aspects, or whether there are obvious errors. You need separate evaluation logic to assess output quality and trigger revision when it falls short.

None of this means language models are not useful. They are the engine of the system. But they need a chassis around them.

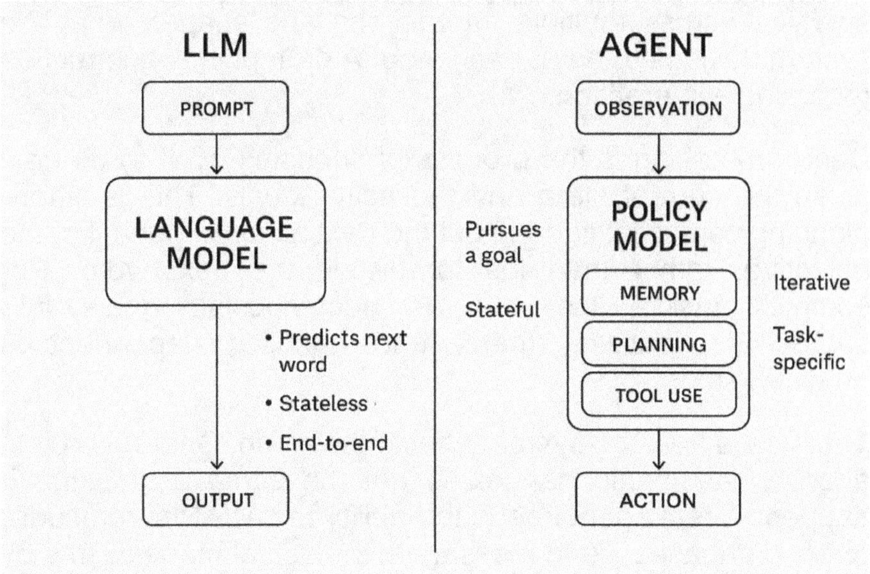

What an Agent Is

The term "agent" has accumulated a lot of baggage in AI discourse, some of it from academic AI research going back decades and some of it from recent marketing. For this book I am using a specific definition: an agent is a system that perceives some state of the world, maintains goals, takes actions to make progress toward those goals, and updates its understanding based on what happens.

That definition has five working parts.

Perception means the system receives information from its environment: user input, API responses, database contents, the output of other agents, whatever is relevant to the current task. Without some form of input, there is nothing to reason about.

Goal representation means the system has some persistent understanding of what it is trying to accomplish. This is where a lot of simple LLM-based systems fall short. They do not really have goals; they have prompts. A goal is something that survives across multiple interactions and shapes what the system decides to do at each step. A prompt is an instruction for a single interaction.

Decision-making is the process of choosing what to do next given the current state and the active goals. This is where planning comes in: figuring out the next action in pursuit of the objective, rather than just predicting the next word. For complex tasks, this involves decomposing goals into subtasks, prioritizing them, and handling dependencies between steps.

Tool use is how the system affects the world. Generating text about what should happen is not the same as making it happen. A real agent needs the ability to call APIs, run code, query databases, send messages: the actual mechanisms by which it can change the state of things outside itself.

Memory is what lets the system maintain continuity across interactions, learn from what has already happened, and avoid repeating work or mistakes. Without memory, every session starts from zero.

When you put these five things together in a coherent architecture, you get something that behaves qualitatively differently from a chatbot or a simple prompt chain. It can work on tasks over extended periods, recover from failures, and build on previous work.

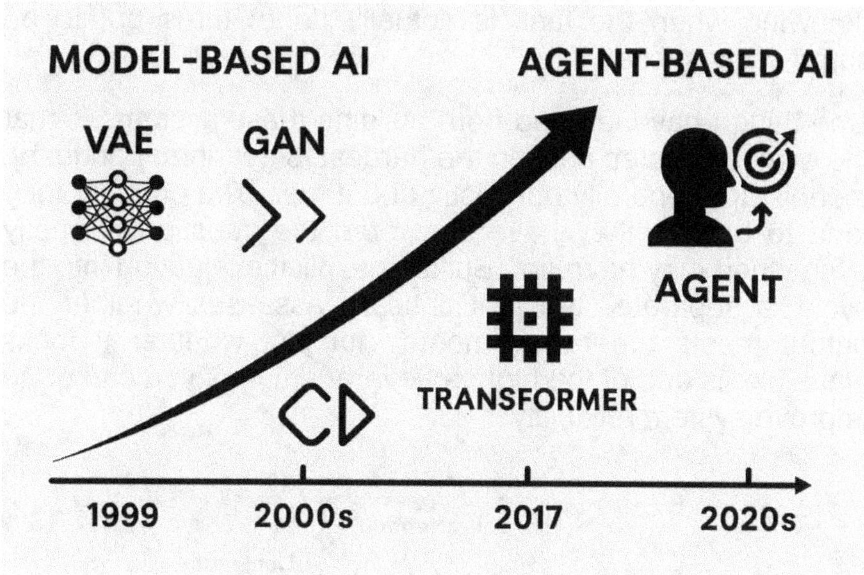

The Cycle Agents Run On

Most useful agents operate through a continuous cycle. They observe the current state, decide on an action, execute that action, observe the result, and repeat until the goal is achieved or some stopping condition is reached.

In practice this looks like: observe whatever input is available (user request, tool output, memory retrieval), decide what action to take given the current goal and state, execute that action (which might mean generating text, calling a tool, or delegating to another agent), incorporate the result into the working state, and check whether the goal has been reached or the plan needs revision.

The cycle is simple in principle and genuinely tricky in practice, mostly because each step has failure modes. Observation can be noisy or incomplete. Planning can be wrong, especially when the model overestimates its own capabilities or makes assumptions about the environment that turn out to be false. Actions can fail in unexpected ways. Memory systems can retrieve the wrong context. Evaluation (knowing when the task is actually done) turns out to be surprisingly subtle.

One thing I have learned from building these systems is that the evaluation step is often the hardest to get right. Language models are generally optimistic about their own outputs: they tend to believe they have answered the question correctly even when they have not. Building explicit evaluation into the cycle, a separate step that critically assesses whether the output meets the requirements, not just whether it looks plausible, is one of the highest-leverage things you can do to improve system reliability.

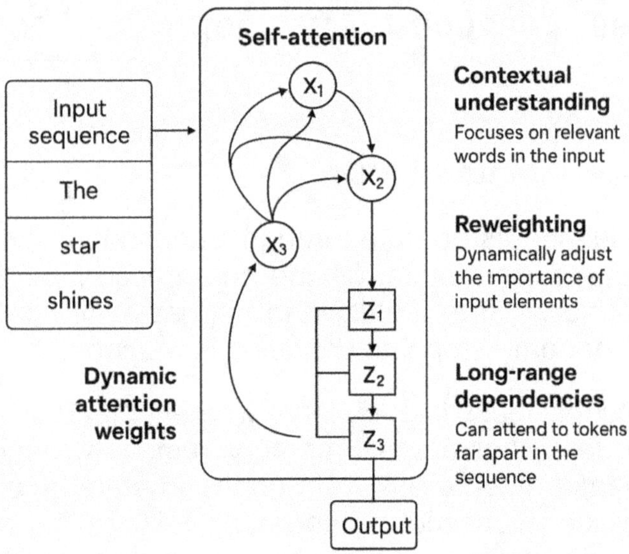

Building Up From a Language Model

If you are starting from a raw language model and want to build something genuinely agentic, there is a rough progression worth following.

The first addition is tools. Give the model the ability to call functions: web search, code execution, database queries, whatever is relevant to your domain. This alone transforms what is possible. The model stops describing what it would do and starts doing it.

The specifics of how you wire up tool calls depend on the model and framework you are using. OpenAI's function calling API, Anthropic's tool use feature, and the tool abstractions in LangChain and LangGraph all work somewhat differently, but the underlying idea is the same: you describe available tools in the prompt or system configuration, the model generates a structured request to call one of those tools, your code executes the call and returns the result, and the model incorporates the result into its next response.

The second addition is memory. At a minimum, this means persisting conversation history so the model has context about what has happened. More sophisticated memory systems separate out different types of information: what happened in this session, what we know about this user's preferences, what we have learned about how to do this task well. Vector databases are the most common tool for semantic retrieval, though for many use cases a simpler key-value store or even well-structured JSON is sufficient.

The third addition is planning. For tasks requiring more than a few steps, you need something that can decompose a high-level goal into a sequence of actions, track progress through that sequence, and revise the plan when things go wrong. This is often where the coordinator pattern comes in: a planning component that breaks the task apart and a set of more specialized components that execute the pieces.

The fourth addition, which is consistently underestimated, is safety and oversight. An agent that runs autonomously needs constraints on what it can do, mechanisms for escalating when it is uncertain, and some form of audit trail so you can understand what happened when things go wrong. Building this in from the start is much easier than retrofitting it after the fact, when you are dealing with a system that has already been deployed and has users depending on it.

These additions interact. A good memory system makes planning easier because the planner has better context to work with. Good planning makes tool use more effective because the right tools are called in the right order with the right parameters. Effective safety mechanisms depend on good observability, which depends on good logging, which is part of the memory system. This is why the architecture of an agentic system matters as much as the quality of the underlying model: the components reinforce each other when they are designed well, and undermine each other when they are not.

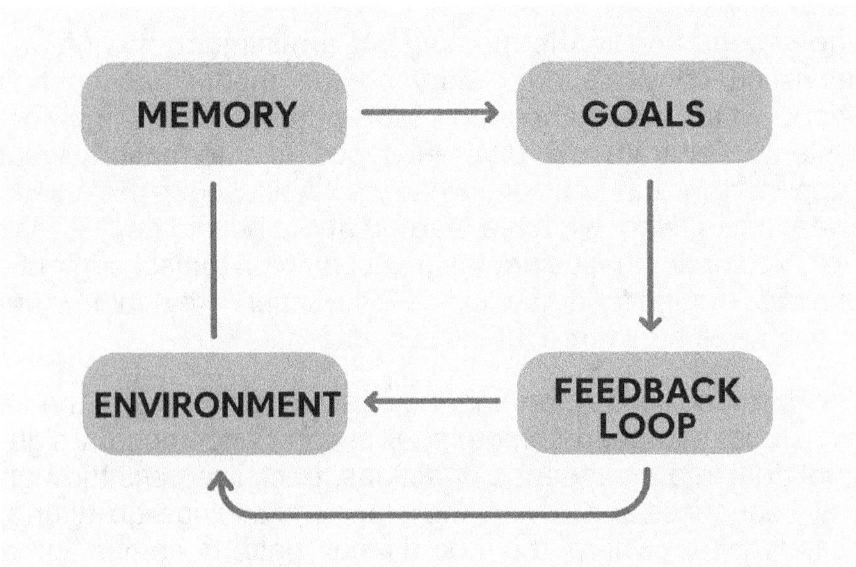

Why the Market Shifted When It Did

In 2022 and early 2023, the dominant production use case for language models was text generation: summarization, content creation, question answering. Real use cases, real value. But two things happened that pushed the field toward agentic approaches.

First, the ceiling on what you could do with a single model call became apparent. For simple tasks, one call is enough. For anything complex, a single call does not cut it, and chaining calls together without real planning and memory leads to fragile systems that break unpredictably. Teams that had built simple prompt chains were hitting these limits and looking for better approaches.

Second, the frameworks matured enough that building agentic systems became feasible for teams without dedicated research infrastructure. LangChain provided modular components for tool use and memory. LangGraph added proper state management for multi-step workflows. CrewAI made multi-agent coordination accessible. AutoGen provided a different model for inter-agent communication. None of these are perfect, but they lowered the barrier enough that practitioners could build real systems without starting from scratch.

Third, the business cases started becoming clearer. Companies that had been running pilots with simple integrations were hitting the same walls: impressive in demos, unreliable in production, unable to handle edge cases, requiring constant human oversight. Agentic architectures, done properly, address some of these problems, if not all of them. The ROI became visible in specific domains: customer service automation, research assistance, content pipeline management, operations monitoring.

There is also something worth acknowledging about the current moment specifically. We are at a point where the frameworks are good enough to build real things, but not so mature that the patterns are fully standardized. This means there is genuine design work involved in building agentic systems, not just configuration. The decisions you make about memory architecture, planning approach, tool design, and oversight mechanisms will significantly affect how well your system works and how maintainable it is over time. That design work is what this book is primarily about.

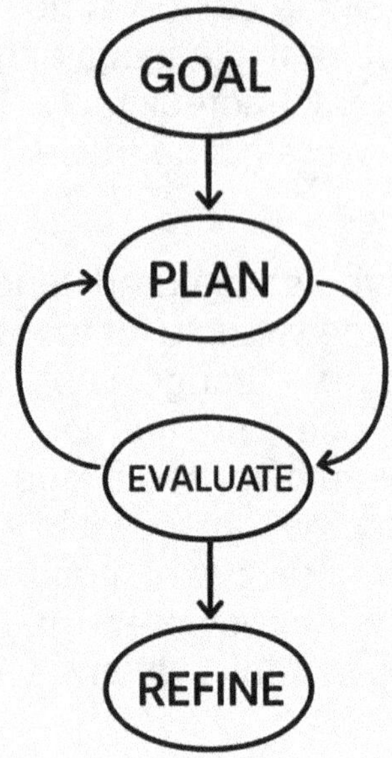

Where This Leaves the Practitioner

Building with language models means accepting some tradeoffs honestly. Hallucinations are real and you need to architect around them rather than hoping the model will not produce them. Models are expensive to run at scale and you need to think carefully about when a language model is the right tool versus a simpler programmatic approach. The field changes fast enough that a system you build today may need significant rework within a year. And autonomous systems that take real-world actions have real-world consequences, so the oversight and safety questions are not optional afterthoughts.

None of that should be paralyzing. The tools are genuinely useful and the potential is real. But I would rather be honest about the tradeoffs than paint an uncomplicated picture that sets you up for disappointment when you hit the inevitable rough edges.

The next chapter gets into what agency, autonomy, and intent actually mean in practice. They are related concepts that play distinct roles in system design, and the distinctions matter more than they might seem at first.

Chapter 2

Agency, Autonomy, and Intent

These three words get used interchangeably in most AI writing, which is part of why conversations about agentic AI can feel so slippery. They are related, but they are not the same thing, and the differences matter when you are actually designing a system.

Agency

Agency is the capacity to take actions in pursuit of goals. That is a broad definition, deliberately so, because the question in practice is never whether something is an agent in some philosophical sense. It is whether it exhibits agency in a particular situation. A thermostat has a tiny bit of agency: it acts on a goal, which is maintaining temperature. A human being has considerably more. For AI systems, agency is mostly about what the system can do and what it is actively trying to accomplish.

An LLM with no tools and no persistent goal has almost none. It processes input and generates output. An LLM with tool access, persistent memory, and a goal it is working toward has considerably more.

The practical question when designing a system is: what decisions is the agent allowed to make on its own, and which ones require a human? That question turns out to be more important than most architectural decisions. Get it wrong in one direction and you have a system that is constantly asking for confirmation and provides no real value over doing things manually. Get it wrong in the other direction and you have a system making consequential decisions it should not be trusted with.

I have found it useful to think about agency as a set of independent dimensions rather than a single dial. There is action scope: the range of things the system can do. There is decision threshold: how much uncertainty triggers escalation to a human. There is time horizon: how far into the future the system is allowed to plan and commit to. And there is reversibility: whether the actions it takes can be undone if something goes wrong.

A customer service agent that can draft emails but requires human approval before sending them has moderate action scope, a low decision threshold, a short time horizon, and high reversibility. That is appropriate for early deployment. As you gain confidence, you might lower the decision threshold and let it send lower-stakes emails automatically, while keeping tight control on action scope so it cannot escalate to legal or initiate refunds without approval. This kind of incremental expansion is much safer than trying to define the full autonomy profile upfront.

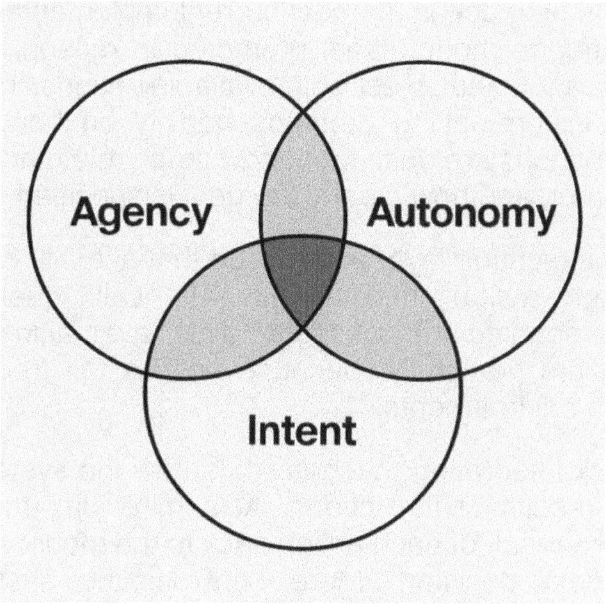

Building Blocks of Agency

To build agency into a system, you need to think carefully about each component. Goal awareness means the system knows what it is trying to accomplish at any given moment, not just in this interaction but in the context of the broader task. This sounds obvious but many systems fail here: they have a prompt that describes a role, but no persistent representation of the specific goal they are currently working toward.

A perception loop means the system can take in information from multiple sources and update its understanding of the current situation. For a research agent, this means being able to read web pages, process API responses, and integrate retrieved documents. For a customer service agent, this means reading the customer's message, accessing their account history, and checking the current policy documentation.

A decision engine is the mechanism by which the system chooses its next action. In most current implementations, this is the language model itself, prompted to reason about the current situation and select from available options. The quality of this decision-making depends heavily on how well the available options are described, how much relevant context is in the prompt, and how clearly the goal is specified.

An action execution layer is the code that actually carries out the chosen action: making the API call, querying the database, sending the message. This layer also needs to handle errors gracefully, because actions fail frequently in production environments.

A feedback integration mechanism is how the system learns from the results of its actions. At a minimum, this means passing the result of each action back to the model as context for the next decision. More sophisticated systems log outcomes and use them to update their approach over time.

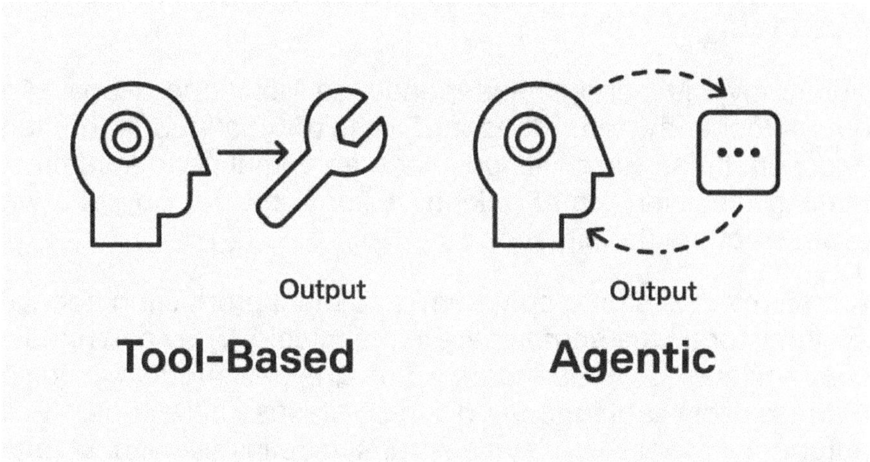

Observable Behaviors That Signal Agency

You know you are seeing agency in action when a system does things you did not explicitly tell it to do when those things are clearly necessary for the goal. If you ask it to prepare a report and it notices a key data source is missing and flags that before proceeding rather than generating a report with obvious gaps, that is agency. If it just generates the report with gaps anyway, it is a sophisticated text processor.

Another signal is how the system handles failure. A reactive model simply returns an error message. An agentic system tries an alternative approach, reports what it tried and why it failed, and asks for guidance if it cannot make progress on its own.

Consistent behavior across similar situations is a third signal. If the system handles the same type of request in dramatically different ways across different sessions, it probably does not have genuine agency: it is pattern-matching on surface features of the input rather than reasoning about how to achieve a goal.

Autonomy

Autonomy is about independence of operation. An autonomous system does not require continuous human direction. It can run on its own for meaningful periods of time, making decisions and taking actions based on its own assessment of the situation.

Autonomy exists on a spectrum, and most production agentic systems today are somewhere in the middle. They can handle common cases independently but are designed to involve humans for ambiguous or high-stakes situations. Full autonomy, where the system runs indefinitely without any human oversight, is appropriate for very narrow and low-stakes tasks and essentially nowhere else right now.

What makes autonomy hard is the trust problem. For a system to run autonomously, you have to trust that its decision-making is good enough across the full range of situations it will encounter, including edge cases you have not thought of. That trust has to be earned through observation, testing, and gradual expansion of the system's operating envelope. Teams that try to go from zero to full autonomy in one step almost always regret it.

The practical architectural implication is that autonomy should be explicitly configured, not implicit. A system that happens to run without human intervention because nobody thought to add oversight mechanisms is very different from a system that has been deliberately designed with defined escalation paths, confidence thresholds, and audit trails. The first will surprise you eventually. The second is built to tell you when it is uncertain.

What Enables Autonomy

A good model alone is not enough. You need to design systems with several specific capabilities for autonomy to work reliably.

Goal retention means the system can maintain its objective across context resets, interruptions, and failures. If the goal lives only in the active context window, every new session or every time the context is cleared, the system loses track of what it was trying to do. Goals should be stored persistently and loaded at the start of each session or each major step.

Event awareness means the system can recognize when it needs to act without being explicitly prompted. An email triage agent should process incoming emails as they arrive, not only when a human tells it to check the inbox. A monitoring agent should detect anomalies and respond to them, not wait to be asked whether anything unusual has happened.

Replanning capability means the system can recognize when its current approach is not working and generate a new plan rather than repeatedly failing in the same way. This requires some form of self-evaluation: the system needs to assess whether it is making progress and decide when to change course.

Graceful escalation means knowing when to stop trying to solve something autonomously and involve a human instead. This is one of the harder capabilities to build because it requires the system to have an accurate model of its own uncertainty, which language models are not naturally good at. Calibrating the escalation threshold requires empirical observation: you want to escalate often enough to catch cases where the system is genuinely confused, but not so often that the human oversight overhead defeats the purpose of having an autonomous system.

Real-World Examples of Scoped Autonomy

An email triage agent can run every ten minutes, classify incoming messages, draft replies for low-stakes inquiries, and escalate anything that seems sensitive or outside its scope. No human prompt is required for each cycle. The human involvement is in defining the scope, reviewing escalated items, and occasionally updating the classification rules when edge cases come up.

An inventory monitoring agent watches stock levels against a defined threshold. When a product falls below the threshold, it checks supplier pricing, verifies the budget is available, and either initiates a reorder automatically or flags the situation for human review depending on the order value. The key design decision is the cutoff between automatic and human-reviewed: setting it based on both order value and supplier reliability rather than just one dimension tends to produce better outcomes.

A content review agent can check new content against policy guidelines, flag potential violations, and route them to human reviewers with a structured summary of the specific concern. It does not make the final decision on borderline cases, but it does the work of identifying and organizing what needs human attention, which is itself valuable.

In each of these cases, the autonomy is useful precisely because it is scoped. The system is not trying to handle everything; it is handling the predictable cases reliably while routing the unpredictable ones to humans who can exercise judgment.

Intent

Intent is the hardest of the three to pin down, and the concept I find most underappreciated in practical system design.

When I talk about intent in an agentic system, I mean the encoded representation of what the system is supposed to be doing. This means the broader purpose, extending beyond the immediate task. A system with good intent representation behaves consistently with its purpose even in situations that were not explicitly anticipated in the design.

The contrast case is a system that is good at following instructions but has no real understanding of what those instructions are for. These systems do what they are told when the instructions are clear, but they fall apart when they hit situations the instructions did not cover. They either fail outright or do something technically compliant but obviously wrong.

Here is a concrete example. You are building a research assistant whose job is to help analysts write reports. The analyst asks it to find recent data on market share in electric vehicles. A system with shallow instruction-following will run a search and return whatever it finds. A system with better intent representation will notice that "recent" probably means the last twelve months given the business context, that market share data should come from credible industry sources rather than blog posts, that the analyst probably needs this formatted in a way that is easy to cite, and that if the data is mixed or contested it should flag that rather than picking one figure and presenting it as definitive.

None of that comes from the specific instruction. It comes from the system having some representation of the broader purpose: what good work looks like in this context, who is asking and why, what the downstream use is.

Building intent into a system is partly about how you structure the system prompt and goal specification. It is also about memory. A system that remembers past interactions with a user builds a richer model of what they are actually trying to accomplish, which lets it serve their real intent rather than their stated request. These are often different.

The Four Layers of Intent

Goal representation is the most explicit layer: what is the system trying to accomplish in concrete terms? This should be specific enough that you could evaluate whether it has been achieved. "Help with research" is too vague. "Provide accurate, well-sourced summaries of specific topics that analysts can directly cite in their reports" is workable.

Priority and value modeling is the next layer: when goals conflict or when there are multiple ways to accomplish something, what principles should guide the choice? A customer service agent might need to balance resolution speed against customer satisfaction against policy compliance. Making these tradeoffs explicit in the design, rather than leaving them implicit in the model's priors, produces more predictable behavior.

Persistence means the goal survives setbacks. If the system encounters an obstacle and simply stops, it probably does not have robust intent representation. A system with genuine intent finds alternative paths, reports what it tried, and maintains its commitment to the goal even when the direct route is blocked.

Contextual alignment is the subtlest layer: does the system's behavior match the spirit of its purpose across situations the designer did not specifically anticipate? This is the layer you discover in production rather than in design, which is why ongoing evaluation is so important. A system that is well-aligned in this sense does sensible things in novel situations. A system that is not aligned does technically permitted things that are clearly wrong.

Measuring Intent Alignment

The practical way to evaluate intent is to observe the system's behavior in situations that were not specifically covered in the design. Does it do sensible things? Does it err in the direction of being helpful rather than being harmful? Does it recognize when it is outside its competence and behave accordingly?

This kind of evaluation requires human judgment and cannot be fully automated, which is one reason why ongoing human involvement in agentic systems is not just a safety precaution but an operational necessity. The system's alignment with its intent only becomes visible through use, and maintaining that alignment requires attention over time as the system encounters new situations.

How the Three Interact

These three concepts interact in ways worth thinking through before you start designing.

High autonomy without good intent is the most dangerous combination. The system acts on its own, but without a solid representation of what it is supposed to be doing, its actions might be technically within scope while completely missing the point. This is not just a theoretical concern. I have seen content generation systems that were optimized for engagement metrics produce content that was technically compliant with their specifications while being actively harmful to the organizations that deployed them.

Good intent without sufficient autonomy means the system cannot act on what it understands. It might correctly identify what needs to be done but still require so much human direction at each step that it provides little value over doing things manually. This happens when teams are too conservative with the decision threshold: they understand the risks of autonomy but have not built enough confidence in the system to start relaxing constraints.

Autonomy and intent without adequate agency means the system plans but cannot act. It might be great at telling you what should be done while being incapable of doing it. Building the tool integrations is often the most unglamorous part of this work, but it is what separates a system that is impressive in a conversation from one that does real work.

The target is calibration across all three: enough agency to do meaningful work in the domain, enough autonomy to operate without constant human oversight for common cases, and an intent representation that keeps the system oriented toward its actual purpose even when instructions are incomplete or ambiguous. Getting there takes iteration, and most of the iteration happens through architectural decisions rather than model improvements.

Chapter 3

Inside an Agentic System: Memory, Goals, Environments, and Feedback

The theoretical framework from the last chapter is useful but abstract. This chapter gets into the actual components of an agentic system, the pieces you're going to build and the ways they interact. I'll try to keep this grounded because the abstractions become clearer once you've seen what they correspond to in actual code.

Memory

I used to underestimate how much of agentic system design is really memory system design. The model is mostly a fixed resource; you can choose which one to use, but you can't change how it works. The tools you integrate are important but relatively straightforward to add. Memory is where the interesting design decisions happen, and getting it wrong is the most common source of failure I've seen in production systems.

The basic problem is this: language models have a context window, a maximum amount of text they can consider at once. Current models are better than they were (some support contexts of 128,000 tokens or more), but context windows are still finite, still expensive to fill, and still degrade in quality at the tails for most practical purposes. A system that runs over multiple sessions, or that needs to draw on information from many past interactions, can't just stuff everything into the context. You need a way to store information persistently and retrieve the relevant parts when they're needed.

Types of Memory

There are four kinds of memory that come up regularly in agentic system design, and they serve different purposes.

Working memory is what's in the current context window: the immediate task, recent conversation turns, any information that's been retrieved in this session. It's fast to access and easy to update, but it's temporary and limited in size. For most agents, working memory is managed implicitly through how you structure the prompt and what you include in each call.

Working memory management is actually one of the subtler arts in agentic system design. With a large context window, the temptation is to include everything that might be relevant. But more context does not always mean better reasoning. Models tend to pay more attention to information near the beginning and end of a prompt than to information in the middle, which means burying important context in the middle of a very long prompt can actually hurt performance. Being selective about what goes into the context, and where it goes, matters.

Episodic memory is the record of what happened: past interactions, completed tasks, decisions made and their outcomes. This is stored externally, usually in a database, and retrieved selectively. It's valuable for personalization (remembering user preferences), for avoiding repeated mistakes, and for long-running tasks where you need to pick up where you left off. The tricky part is deciding what to store, since not everything is worth keeping, and how to retrieve it effectively when you need it.

One design principle that has served me well: store episodic memory in a form that's useful for future decisions, not just as a record of what happened. Instead of storing "user asked about X and I answered Y," store "user asked about X; the answer that worked was Y; the answer that didn't work was Z; key context was A, B, C." This extra structure makes retrieved episodic memories more actionable.

Semantic memory is general knowledge: facts about the world, about the domain you're operating in, about the users you serve. This is typically stored in a vector database and retrieved through semantic similarity search. The key design decision is what to embed: documents, facts, examples, or some combination. Retrieval quality matters enormously because retrieved context that's irrelevant or misleading is often worse than no context at all.

Procedural memory is knowledge about how to do things: workflows, successful approaches, learned heuristics. This is the least standardized type and different systems handle it differently. Some encode it in the system prompt, some store it in memory that gets retrieved alongside task descriptions, some use it to fine-tune the underlying model. The right approach depends on how frequently the procedures are used and how stable they are.

In practice, most production agents use all four types to some degree, with different storage backends and retrieval strategies for each. The architecture can get complex, and complexity has costs: more moving parts means more things that can go wrong and more latency. Start with the simplest memory architecture that serves your use case and add complexity only when you've identified a specific gap.

One thing worth being explicit about: the quality of your memory system is often more important than the quality of your model. I've worked with systems where switching from GPT-3.5 to GPT-4 produced marginal improvement, but improving the retrieval strategy for long-term memory produced a step change in usefulness. The model is already pretty good. Whether it has the right context to work with is frequently the bottleneck.

Common Failures

A few memory failures come up so often they're worth naming specifically.

Memory pollution is when irrelevant or incorrect information gets retrieved and included in the context. The model tends to reason over everything that's in the context, so bad memory retrieval leads to bad reasoning. The fix is usually better indexing, better retrieval queries, or adding a filtering step that evaluates relevance before including something.

I've seen memory pollution cause subtle failures that are hard to diagnose. The model produces outputs that seem slightly off, but there's no obvious error. Tracing it back to a specific piece of polluting context requires detailed logging of what was retrieved and when. This is one reason logging memory retrievals alongside model outputs is worth the overhead.

Memory staleness is when the system is working from outdated information: a user's preferences from six months ago, a fact that's changed since it was stored. You need explicit handling for information that expires, either time-based or event-triggered. This is particularly important in domains where information changes frequently, like pricing, inventory, or regulatory requirements.

Memory conflicts arise when two pieces of stored information contradict each other. Without explicit conflict resolution, the model may try to reconcile them or pick one arbitrarily. Building in consistency checks and clear precedence rules saves a lot of confusion. A simple rule like "more recent information takes precedence over older information, unless explicitly flagged as permanent" handles a large fraction of conflicts.

Finally, there's the retrieval miss problem: the system fails to retrieve information that would have been relevant. This is often an embedding quality issue, or a mismatch between how information was indexed and how it's queried. Evaluation of retrieval quality is something a lot of teams skip and almost always wish they hadn't.

Goals

If memory is often underestimated, goals are often handled with insufficient rigor. Most systems I see represent goals as strings in a system prompt. That works for simple cases, but it breaks down as soon as you need to track partial progress, handle goal conflicts, or pick up a task after an interruption.

A goal, for these purposes, is a representation of some desired future state along with enough context to know whether that state has been achieved. A good goal representation needs to be specific enough that the system can evaluate whether it's been reached. "Improve the user experience" is not a goal; it's an aspiration. "Reduce the average number of steps required to complete task X by 30%" is a goal.

Goals need to be persistent across context resets. If the goal lives only in the context window, every new session starts from scratch. Goals should be stored externally and loaded at the start of each session.

Complex goals need to be decomposable. The parent goal "generate a comprehensive market analysis report" decomposes into subgoals around data gathering, analysis, writing, and review, each of which has its own completion criteria.

Systems handling multiple concurrent goals need goals to be prioritized relative to each other. Priority is often implicit but should be explicit.

One pattern that's worked well for me is representing goals as structured objects rather than natural language strings. Something like a JSON structure with fields for the goal description, success criteria, priority, deadline, parent goal, subgoals, and current status. The overhead of maintaining this structure pays off quickly in complex tasks because it makes the planning problem much more tractable.

The other key insight about goals is that they change. Users update their requirements. New information becomes available. Dependencies fail and subgoals become unachievable. A system that can only execute a fixed plan is much less useful than one that can recognize when a plan needs revision and generate a new one.

Goal Completion Detection

One aspect of goal management that deserves more attention than it usually gets is completion detection: how does the system know when it's done?

For simple goals, completion is obvious. For complex goals, it can be surprisingly ambiguous. "Summarize this document" sounds clear until the document is 200 pages long, covers a dozen distinct topics, and the user hasn't specified how long the summary should be. A system that produces a two-sentence summary for a 200-page technical report technically completed the task but probably did not achieve the actual intent.

Building explicit completion criteria into goal specifications, and having the system verify against those criteria before declaring success, produces much better results. "Generate a summary that covers all major sections, is under 500 words, and includes at least one specific example from each section" is a goal that a system can actually evaluate against.

When explicit completion criteria are not available, having the system propose its own interpretation of what "done" looks like and get confirmation before proceeding is a useful pattern. This adds a round-trip but prevents the frustrating scenario where the system declares success on a task the user considers incomplete.

Environment Modeling

Every agent operates in an environment: the context within which it perceives and acts. Understanding that environment well is necessary for making good decisions, and yet it's often something that teams don't think carefully about until something goes wrong.

The environment includes the obvious stuff: what tools are available, what data sources can be accessed, what constraints apply. But it also includes things that are easy to overlook.

Time is part of the environment. When is it? What deadlines apply? Is this a situation where a decision needs to be made right now or can it wait? A lot of agentic failures I've seen come from systems that are temporally naive: they don't track when things happen and so can't reason about urgency or sequencing. Including the current timestamp in the context for time-sensitive tasks is a small change that prevents a significant class of errors.

The system's own state is part of the environment. What has already been tried in this session? What's pending? What failed? This is different from memory of past interactions; it's the immediate operational context. Systems that don't track their own state end up repeating actions, missing dependencies, and failing to notice when they're stuck in a loop.

The user is part of the environment, and often the most important part. What role are they playing? What do they know? What are they trying to accomplish beyond what they've stated explicitly? Good agents model the user to some degree, treating them as an entity with context, goals, and constraints rather than just a source of instructions.

Resource constraints are part of the environment. Tokens have a cost. API calls take time. Some operations are irreversible. An agent that ignores resource constraints will work well in testing and blow up in production. Building in explicit cost awareness is good practice.

Modeling the environment well usually means encoding it explicitly rather than hoping the model figures it out from context. A structured representation of what tools are available with their costs, latency characteristics, and failure modes, what the current state is, what constraints apply, and who is asking and why: this is the kind of scaffolding that makes the difference between a system that works reliably and one that works mostly.

Environmental Uncertainty

One thing I've learned to build for explicitly is environmental uncertainty: situations where the agent doesn't know something about the environment that it needs to know in order to proceed.

A system that proceeds confidently in the face of environmental uncertainty will often produce wrong outputs. A system that recognizes uncertainty and either gathers the missing information or flags the uncertainty to the user produces much better outcomes, even if it's slower.

Building in uncertainty detection, having the system explicitly identify what it doesn't know that it needs to know, and designing appropriate responses (query the missing information, ask the user, or proceed with a clearly flagged assumption) is worth the implementation effort.

Feedback Loops

I've left feedback until last, partly because it's the component that most distinguishes production systems from demos.

A demo succeeds when it works on the cases you've prepared. A production system succeeds when it keeps working on cases you haven't prepared, which means it needs to learn from what happens and adjust. Feedback loops are how that adjustment happens.

The simplest form of feedback is logging. If you log what the system did, what inputs it received, and what outputs it generated, you can audit its behavior and identify patterns of failure. This is not glamorous, but it is foundational.

The next level is explicit evaluation: building mechanisms that assess output quality and flag problems. This can be a separate LLM call that reviews the agent's output against quality criteria, a rule-based check for common failure modes, or human review on sampled outputs.

Active learning from feedback means the system can actually update its behavior based on what it learns, without requiring a model retrain. This usually happens through memory: storing successful approaches and retrieving them for similar tasks, storing failure cases and using them as negative examples.

The hardest part of feedback loop design is deciding what signals to trust. Explicit user feedback is valuable but sparse. Implicit signals are richer but require interpretation. Getting this right takes experimentation, and the right signals vary significantly by use case.

One principle that's held up well: systems should be designed to fail informatively. When something goes wrong, the failure should produce enough information to diagnose the cause.

Putting It Together

A week ago I watched a junior developer on my team debug a production issue with one of our agents. The system had been working well for a month and then started producing noticeably worse outputs without any obvious trigger. It took about three hours to trace it back to a change in one of our data sources that caused the memory retrieval to start returning stale context: information from before the change that contradicted the current state.

The fix was straightforward once we found it. But the fact that it took three hours to find is instructive. We had good logging. We had evaluation metrics. What we didn't have was a clear link between the retrieval behavior and the output quality metrics. Adding that link, a simple correlation between what the memory system returned and how good the output was, would have pointed us to the problem in minutes.

Every production system has lessons like this built into it. The frameworks get better, the models get better, but the fundamental challenge of building reliable systems that operate on real-world data in real-world conditions stays fundamentally the same. Memory, goals, environment modeling, and feedback loops are the tools. Using them well is the craft.

Chapter 4

The Models Underneath: From VAEs to Transformers

I want to spend a chapter on the generative model landscape, not because you need to understand all of it in depth to build agentic systems, but because you'll encounter these terms constantly and it helps to know roughly what they mean and how they relate to each other.

The short version: the transformer architecture, introduced in 2017, is responsible for almost everything that matters for agentic AI. The other architectures, VAEs, GANs, diffusion models, are worth knowing about because they appear in multimodal contexts and because they illustrate how the field got here, but they're not what you'll be working with day to day.

Variational Autoencoders

A VAE is an older architecture designed to learn compressed representations of data. The core idea is to train two networks together: an encoder that compresses input into a compact "latent" representation, and a decoder that reconstructs the original input from that representation. The "variational" part means the latent space is structured probabilistically, which makes it possible to generate new samples by drawing from the learned distribution rather than just reconstructing existing inputs.

VAEs produce plausible but often blurry outputs. For images, they tend to smooth over details in ways that look unnatural. For text, they were never that competitive with other approaches. Their main value today is in domains where interpretability of the latent space matters, certain drug discovery applications, for example, and in research on disentangled representations, where the goal is to learn a latent space where different dimensions correspond to meaningful independent factors.

The connection to agentic AI is conceptual more than practical. VAEs showed that you could learn structured representations of complex data in ways that support generation and manipulation, going beyond simple recognition. The idea of a meaningful latent space, where similar things are close together and you can interpolate between them, shows up in how we think about embedding spaces in modern retrieval systems. When you store documents in a vector database and retrieve them by semantic similarity, you're working with a latent space that serves a similar conceptual function.

GANs and StyleGAN

Generative Adversarial Networks were the image generation technology of choice for several years before diffusion models took over. The basic setup involves two networks in competition: a generator that tries to produce realistic images, and a discriminator that tries to tell real images from generated ones. Training them against each other pushes both toward better performance.

GANs could produce very sharp, realistic images, much sharper than VAEs, but they were notoriously difficult to train, prone to mode collapse (producing only a narrow range of outputs), and hard to control. StyleGAN, developed by NVIDIA, addressed some of the control problems by restructuring the generator to separate high-level style from fine-grained detail, allowing manipulation of specific attributes without affecting others.

If you're building a content generation pipeline that includes image generation, you're probably using diffusion models today, not GANs. But understanding GANs helps with the intuition for how adversarial training works, which comes up in contexts like adversarial robustness testing for AI systems and in certain training approaches for language models.

The broader lesson from the GAN era is about the importance of having a learning signal that captures what you actually care about. The discriminator in a GAN provides a training signal that's much richer than simple reconstruction loss, which is part of why GANs produce sharper outputs than VAEs. This insight, that the quality of the learning signal matters as much as the architecture, carries forward into how we think about fine-tuning language models on human feedback.

Diffusion Models

Diffusion models are the current dominant approach for image generation, powering Stable Diffusion, DALL-E, and Midjourney. The basic idea is to train a model to reverse a gradual noising process: given a slightly noisy version of an image, predict the slightly less noisy version. By chaining together many small denoising steps, you can generate an image from pure noise.

Diffusion models are easier to train than GANs, produce high-quality outputs, and support more controllable generation through techniques like classifier-free guidance. They're also substantially slower than GANs because the generation process requires many sequential denoising steps.

For agentic systems, diffusion models matter primarily in multimodal contexts. An agent that can generate images as part of its outputs, or that needs to interpret images as part of its inputs, will interact with diffusion-based or diffusion-adjacent systems. Understanding roughly how they work helps when you're debugging generation artifacts or trying to understand why a particular control technique is or isn't working.

The Transformer

The transformer is the architecture that powers GPT-4, Claude, Gemini, and essentially every high-performing language model. It was introduced in a 2017 Google paper called "Attention Is All You Need," which turned out to be almost literally true. The architecture based on attention mechanisms has scaled much better than its predecessors and become the foundation of the current generation of AI.

The key innovation is the attention mechanism, which lets the model compute relationships between any two positions in the input simultaneously rather than processing sequentially from left to right. This is what allows transformers to capture long-range dependencies in text and to parallelize computation across the whole input.

The high-level intuition is useful even if you don't go into the mathematical details. When you're processing a sentence, different words matter different amounts for understanding any given word. "The trophy doesn't fit in the suitcase because it's too big": understanding what "it" refers to requires comparing it to both "trophy" and "suitcase" and using contextual clues to resolve the ambiguity. Attention provides a learned mechanism for doing exactly this kind of comparison.

What made transformers especially powerful in practice was that they scaled. As you add more parameters and train on more data, performance keeps improving in predictable ways. This property, which earlier architectures lacked, meant that the main lever for better language models was just making them bigger and training them longer. The result is GPT-4, Claude, and their peers, which have capabilities that would have seemed implausible a decade ago.

Understanding Scaling

The scaling behavior of transformers has some practical implications worth understanding.

Larger models are generally better at tasks that require broad knowledge, complex reasoning, and handling novel situations. Smaller models are faster, cheaper, and often good enough for well-defined, narrow tasks. Knowing when to reach for a larger model versus a smaller one is a practical skill that affects both cost and quality.

Fine-tuning a smaller model on domain-specific data can often produce better results for narrow tasks than prompting a larger general model. But fine-tuning requires data, compute, and careful evaluation, so the tradeoff only makes sense when the task volume is high enough to justify the investment.

The relationship between model size and capability is not always intuitive. Some capabilities seem to emerge somewhat suddenly as models get larger, appearing in larger models but not in smaller ones even when the smaller models perform adequately on many other tasks. Being aware of this means being appropriately cautious about assuming that a smaller model will handle edge cases the same way a larger one does.

Context Length

For agentic systems specifically, the properties that matter most start with context length. The amount of text the model can consider at once has grown from a few thousand tokens to hundreds of thousands in current models. This directly affects how much working memory the agent has available and how long the conversation history it can consider.

Longer context is generally useful, but it's not without tradeoffs. Very long contexts can be expensive to process. They can also cause subtle quality degradation for information that appears in the middle of a very long input, since models tend to pay more attention to the beginning and end of context. Managing what goes into the context window and where remains important even as context windows get larger.

Instruction Following

Through fine-tuning on human feedback, these models have become very good at following complex instructions and maintaining consistent behavior across a conversation. This is what makes it feasible to build agents with defined roles and responsibilities.

The quality of instruction following varies across models and tasks. For tasks that closely resemble what's in the fine-tuning data, instruction following is generally excellent. For novel combinations of requirements, there can be surprising failures. Testing instruction following on the specific task types your agent needs to handle, rather than assuming general capability, is worth doing before committing to a particular model.

Function Calling and Tool Use

Models like GPT-4 can be fine-tuned or prompted to generate structured outputs that can be parsed as function calls.

Combined with an orchestration layer that actually executes those calls, this is the foundation of agentic tool use.

Different models have different reliability characteristics for function calling. Some are more consistent about generating well-formed tool calls; others are more prone to generating malformed parameters or calling tools in inappropriate contexts. Evaluating these characteristics specifically for your use case, rather than relying on general benchmarks, gives you a more accurate picture of what to expect in production.

Reasoning

Through techniques like chain-of-thought prompting, these models can be guided to work through problems step by step rather than jumping directly to an answer. The quality of this reasoning is impressive for some tasks and clearly lacking for others. Mathematics and formal logic remain areas where language models make characteristic mistakes even when reasoning in steps. Knowing the limits of language model reasoning is important for deciding where to trust the model's judgment and where to add additional verification.

Multimodal Transformers

The transformer architecture has extended beyond text. GPT-4V, Gemini, and other multimodal models can process images alongside text, which opens up agentic applications that weren't previously possible.

A document processing agent that can read scanned PDFs becomes much more useful when it can handle image-heavy reports, diagrams, and charts. A monitoring agent can analyze screenshots of dashboards rather than requiring structured data exports. A customer service agent can understand product images that customers send in alongside their questions.

Worth noting: multimodal capability is sometimes used in demos in ways that don't hold up in production. Image understanding is generally less reliable than text understanding, particularly for tasks requiring precise extraction of information from complex visuals. Build in validation and fallback paths when you're relying on it.

How This Matters Practically

For most agentic system builders, the choice of underlying model is a practical question. The major providers offer similar capabilities at roughly similar price points, with some differences in context length, multimodal capability, structured output support, and fine-tuning options. The factors worth evaluating are context length, function calling reliability, cost, latency, and fine-tuning support.

The underlying architecture will keep evolving. Right now, transformers and attention mechanisms dominate. But the concepts around memory, planning, tool use, and goal representation that we've been discussing don't depend on the specific architecture. They'll remain relevant whatever the next generation of models looks like.

Chapter 5

Language as the Interface Layer

There's something genuinely strange about building systems where language is both the input and the control mechanism. We're used to programming computers by writing precise instructions in formal languages where every symbol has exactly one meaning. Natural language is almost the opposite: ambiguous, context-dependent, with meaning that shifts based on who's speaking and what they already know.

And yet here we are, building systems where the way you write the prompt is as important as the code around it, where the "language layer" is doing work that in previous generations would have required explicit logic, and where figuring out how to express a task in words is a core engineering skill.

This chapter is about why that works, what it means for how you design agentic systems, and where the language interface is genuinely useful versus where it introduces problems you'd be better off solving with explicit code.

Token Prediction as Thought Simulation

Language models predict the next token given the preceding tokens. That's the literal description of what they do. The question is why doing that at massive scale, on enormous text corpora, produces something that can reason, plan, and generalize in ways the explicit objective doesn't seem to require.

The answer, as best we understand it, is that predicting text accurately requires building a model of the world good enough to predict what a person who understood that world would say next. To predict "The trophy doesn't fit in the suitcase because it's too ___" correctly, you need to have built something that represents physical objects, their properties, how they relate to each other, and how those relationships affect what people say about them.

Scaled up across essentially the entire written output of human civilization, you get a model that has absorbed an enormous amount about how the world works, how people reason about it, and how they communicate that reasoning. Not perfectly: these models have well-documented failure modes and blind spots. But surprisingly well.

For agentic systems, this matters because it means you can communicate complex intentions to the model through language rather than having to encode them in formal logic. You can say "when summarizing, prefer bullet points for factual information and prose for nuanced analysis" and the model will do something sensible with that, without you having to define what counts as factual versus nuanced. The model has absorbed enough about how people think and write that it can interpret instructions with a degree of contextual sensitivity that would be essentially impossible to achieve through explicit rules.

The flip side is that this flexibility comes with unreliability. The model's interpretation of an instruction can vary based on other things in the context, it can be swayed by patterns that superficially resemble what you asked for but aren't quite right, and it can confidently produce outputs that are wrong in ways that don't match any simple rule you could write to catch them. Understanding this tradeoff is fundamental to designing language-based systems well.

How Language Models Fail

Before getting into how to use language effectively as a control mechanism, it's worth understanding the characteristic ways language models fail, because these failure modes should shape how you design around the language interface.

Hallucination is the most widely discussed failure mode: the model generates plausible-sounding information that isn't true. This happens because the model is optimizing for plausible next tokens, not for factual accuracy. In agentic contexts, hallucination is particularly dangerous because the model may hallucinate tool capabilities, make up data that should be retrieved from a real source, or fabricate steps in a plan that don't actually accomplish the goal.

Sycophancy is a subtler problem: the model tends to agree with the user and confirm their assumptions even when they're wrong. If you say "I think X is the right approach here, what do you think?" the model is more likely to say "yes, X is a good approach" than to push back. This is a significant problem for agentic systems because it means the model may not flag problems with the user's plan even when it should.

Instruction drift is what happens when a model in a long conversation starts diverging from the instructions in its system prompt, gradually being pulled in a different direction by the conversation history. This is especially problematic for agents that run for extended periods. Periodically reinforcing critical instructions, and monitoring for behavioral drift, is worth building in.

Context sensitivity failures occur when the model's behavior changes unexpectedly based on apparently irrelevant context. Adding an example of an unusual edge case to a prompt can cause the model to treat normal cases more like that edge case. Changing the order of instructions can change which ones the model follows most reliably. These effects are hard to predict and require empirical testing to discover.

Language as Control

The system prompt in an agentic application is doing something more than setting context: it's defining the agent's identity, capabilities, constraints, and decision-making principles. Writing a good system prompt is, in a real sense, programming. The difference from traditional programming is that you're working with a system that will try to infer your intent, which has advantages (you don't need to specify every case explicitly) and disadvantages (the system may infer wrong, especially for edge cases).

Some things I've learned about system prompt design:

Be concrete about what success looks like, not just what to do. "Provide helpful responses" is almost useless. "Your answers should be specific enough that a person with no background in this area could act on them without asking follow-up questions" is more useful. "If you're uncertain whether the user has relevant background, ask one clarifying question before answering" is even more useful because it handles a specific failure mode explicitly.

Specify the persona and voice. The way the agent communicates: formal or conversational, concise or thorough, confident or hedging, has a big effect on user experience and varies significantly based on how you describe it. Being explicit is worth it.

Handle the edge cases you know about. If you know users frequently ask questions outside the agent's scope, write explicit instructions for how to handle those. If there's a common misunderstanding about what the agent does, address it. This is much more reliable than hoping the model figures it out.

Don't try to handle everything through the system prompt. Long, over-specified system prompts tend to degrade performance. The model pays less attention to instructions that appear deep in a long context, and dense specifications can conflict with each other in ways that produce erratic behavior. The system prompt should handle the stable, general principles. Specific task instructions often work better as part of the immediate context.

System Prompt Iteration

System prompts require iteration, not just initial design. The first version of a system prompt almost never performs as well as you'd like across the full range of inputs the system encounters.

A practical process: start with a system prompt that covers the core requirements, deploy it to a test environment, collect outputs on a diverse set of inputs, identify failure modes, and update the prompt to address them. Repeat this cycle until the system behaves well across the range of inputs you care about.

The tricky part is that fixing one failure mode sometimes introduces another. Adding an instruction to handle an edge case can inadvertently change behavior for the common cases. Regression testing, maintaining a set of test cases for behaviors you care about and checking that they still pass after each prompt update, helps catch these regressions.

Version control for prompts is worth doing. Keeping track of what changed between prompt versions and what effect the changes had makes the iteration process much more efficient and prevents the disorienting situation of not knowing whether a behavioral change was intentional.

Planning Through Language

Language models can plan, in a limited but often sufficient sense. If you give a model a complex goal and ask it to break it into steps, or to identify what information it needs before proceeding, or to evaluate whether its current approach is working, it can do these things with surprising competence.

Chain-of-thought prompting, asking the model to show its reasoning before arriving at a conclusion, is a simple technique that often significantly improves output quality on tasks that require multi-step reasoning. The improvement is partly because working through the reasoning explicitly helps the model get to the right answer, and partly because the visible reasoning gives you a way to catch errors before they propagate.

More sophisticated planning involves having the model generate a structured plan (often as JSON or a similar format), then executing that plan through a series of calls. The model generates the plan, your code executes each step and feeds the results back in, and the model either proceeds to the next step or updates the plan based on what happened.

This works better than it probably should given that the model has no execution environment of its own. The key is providing enough context in each call for the model to understand where it is in the plan and what needs to happen next, without having to hold the entire plan in the active context for the whole duration of the task.

For long-running tasks, having the model periodically summarize its current state saves context. Not the full history, but the current goal, what's been accomplished, what's remaining, and any relevant observations from the work so far. This summary becomes the seed for subsequent calls, keeping the context manageable while preserving continuity.

Where Language Interface Falls Short

Language-based control is convenient but not always appropriate. A few situations where explicit logic is better:

When precision matters more than flexibility. If a task requires exact specifications, explicit code is more reliable than language instructions.

When the task is simple and stereotyped. Using a language model for something a simple if-else statement could handle adds latency, cost, and a source of variability you don't need.

When you need determinism. Language model outputs are stochastic. For tasks where you need guaranteed consistent behavior, this is a problem.

When performance constraints are tight. Language model calls add hundreds of milliseconds of latency. In time-sensitive contexts, this may be unacceptable.

The error I see most often is using language model calls everywhere because they're convenient, even when simpler approaches would be more reliable and efficient. The agent architecture should use language where language's flexibility and generalization are genuinely valuable, and use explicit logic or rules everywhere else.

Prompt Injection and Security

There's a security concern specific to language-based systems that deserves explicit attention: prompt injection.

Prompt injection is when user-provided content or content retrieved from external sources contains text that influences the model's behavior in unintended ways. A user might embed instructions in their message that cause the model to behave differently than intended. Retrieved web content might contain text that looks like system instructions and causes the model to follow them.

This is a genuine security concern for agentic systems, particularly for agents that retrieve content from external sources or process user-provided documents. Mitigations include: clearly delimiting user-provided content from system instructions in the prompt structure, using structured input formats where the model is less likely to treat content as instructions, and monitoring for unusual behavior that might indicate an injection attempt.

The Role of Language in Multi-Agent Systems

When multiple agents communicate with each other, they typically do so through language. One agent generates a message, another receives and processes it. This is natural given that language models are the substrate, but it introduces some challenges worth anticipating.

Natural language messages between agents are ambiguous in the same ways that natural language messages from humans are. "Continue with the previous approach" means different things depending on what the previous approach was, which requires context that may not be available to the receiving agent. Structured formats, JSON with defined schemas, explicit field names, validation, reduce this ambiguity at the cost of some flexibility.

Agents can also mislead each other, either through honest errors (one agent believes something false and passes it to another) or through failure modes that look like overconfidence (an agent asserts something it isn't sure about). Building in explicit uncertainty representation and having agents flag when they're working from inference rather than direct knowledge reduces this problem.

Inter-agent communication can also be expensive if agents produce verbose outputs. Building in norms for concise, structured communication between agents, as opposed to the richer natural language appropriate for human-facing outputs, is worth doing early in a multi-agent system's design.

Testing Language-Based Systems

Testing systems that use language as their control mechanism requires different approaches than testing traditional software.

Unit tests are harder to write because outputs are probabilistic and vary across runs. What you can test reliably is that outputs fall within acceptable ranges: that a classification is one of the expected categories, that a summary is shorter than the original, that a plan contains the required sections. Testing exact output content is usually fragile.

Behavioral tests are more useful: does the system do the right thing in a given scenario? This requires defining "the right thing" clearly enough to evaluate programmatically, which is itself a valuable exercise.

Adversarial testing, deliberately trying to get the system to fail, often reveals failure modes that don't show up in normal testing. Edge cases, unusual phrasing, topics near the edge of the system's scope: these are where systems tend to fail in production, so testing for them explicitly is worth the effort.

Introduction Additional Content

The Landscape of Current Frameworks

One thing I want to address directly is the explosion of frameworks in this space. When I started building agentic systems, LangChain was new, LangGraph barely existed, and CrewAI and AutoGen were not yet public. By the time you read this, there will likely be frameworks I've never heard of, and some of the ones I mention may have been superseded.

This churn is real and it's a legitimate source of frustration for practitioners. I've had to rewrite parts of production systems when frameworks made breaking changes. I've spent days debugging behavior that turned out to be a bug in the framework rather than in my code. I've made architecture decisions based on framework capabilities that later changed.

The way I've come to think about this: frameworks are scaffolding, not foundations. The architectural patterns, the memory design, the governance approach, the evaluation methodology: these are the foundation and they don't change when a framework releases version 2.0. The specific API calls and class names that implement these patterns: these are scaffolding, and they will change.

Designing systems where the core logic is decoupled from the specific framework implementation is worth the extra effort. It makes migrations easier, tests simpler to write, and the system easier to reason about. It also makes it easier to adopt new frameworks incrementally rather than having to rewrite everything at once.

What to Read Alongside This Book

I've deliberately avoided going deep into topics that are well-covered by other resources, so it's worth flagging what those are.

For the mathematical foundations of transformers and attention mechanisms, the original "Attention Is All You Need" paper by Vaswani et al. is still the best starting point, and the "Illustrated Transformer" blog post by Jay Alammar makes it visually accessible.

For practical LLM prompting beyond what I cover here, the Anthropic prompt engineering guide and OpenAI's cookbook are current and practical.

For deep dives into specific frameworks: the LangGraph documentation is thorough and the examples are well-designed; CrewAI's getting-started guide covers the fundamentals quickly; the AutoGen documentation is more research-oriented but covers multi-agent coordination in depth.

For the safety and alignment dimensions that I cover at a practical level: the AI Safety Fundamentals curriculum covers the theory in depth, and the Partnership on AI's resources address operational safety for deployed systems.

Chapter 1 Additional Content: The History That Led Here

Understanding why agentic systems became practically possible when they did requires a brief look at the path that led here. This isn't ancient history; most of it happened in the last decade.

The early language models, models like GPT-2, were genuinely impressive at text generation but too limited in capability and too expensive to serve at scale to be the basis of autonomous systems. The step change came with GPT-3 in 2020, which demonstrated that scale alone could produce remarkable emergent capabilities. Suddenly models that had never been explicitly taught to do many tasks could do them surprisingly well when prompted correctly.

But GPT-3 and its immediate successors were still primarily text generators. The key developments that enabled agentic applications came in 2022 and 2023: instruction tuning and RLHF (reinforcement learning from human feedback) made models much better at following complex instructions rather than just generating plausible text; function calling features enabled structured output that could be parsed as tool calls; the context window grew large enough to hold extended conversation history; and the cost per token dropped to a point where multi-step agent workflows became economically viable.

These changes didn't happen in isolation from the framework ecosystem. As model capabilities grew, the frameworks matured to take advantage of them. LangChain provided the first widely-used abstractions for tool use and memory management. LangGraph, which came later, addressed the limitations that became apparent when people tried to build complex conditional workflows with the earlier LangChain patterns. Each framework generation both responded to and enabled the next step in what was practically buildable.

The current generation of agentic frameworks represents a relatively mature moment: the core patterns are well-understood, the documentation is reasonable, and there's enough production experience to know what works and what doesn't. This won't last indefinitely; there will be another step change in capability that requires new patterns and new tools. But right now is a good time to build, because the tools are capable and the patterns are understood.

Chapter 2 Additional Content: Agency in Practice

The Minimal Viable Agent

What's the minimum viable agent? This is a useful question to ask because it clarifies what's truly essential versus what's additional capability.

The answer, in my view: a minimal viable agent needs a goal, at least one tool, and the ability to decide when it's done. Everything else, memory, planning, reflection, multi-agent coordination, adds value but isn't strictly required for something to qualify as an agent.

This minimal definition is useful because it gives you a concrete starting point for building. If you're starting a new agentic project, start with the minimum: define the goal clearly, give the agent one or two essential tools, define what "done" looks like, and build from there. Adding complexity before you understand the basic system behavior leads to complex systems that are hard to debug.

I've seen many teams build elaborate multi-agent architectures for problems that would have been solved adequately by a single agent with three tools. The lure of complexity is real in this field; the more moving parts, the more interesting the engineering. But the right amount of complexity is the minimum that produces the required behavior.

Agency and Responsibility

There's a dimension of agency that doesn't fit neatly into the technical framework but is worth naming: agency implies responsibility. When a system has agency, it makes decisions, and decisions have consequences. Who is responsible for those consequences?

The legal and ethical frameworks for answering this question are still being worked out. Current consensus: the organization that deploys an agentic system is responsible for its behavior. The model provider bears some responsibility for the capabilities they've enabled. Individual users are responsible for how they configure and use the system.

For practitioners, this means: when you deploy an agentic system, you're taking on responsibility for what it does. That should inform how carefully you design the governance, how thoroughly you test, and how seriously you take the ongoing operation. These aren't just technical decisions; they're decisions about what your organization is willing to be accountable for.

Chapter 3 Additional Content: Memory in Multi-Session Tasks

When a single task spans multiple sessions, perhaps because it's complex enough to require multiple work sessions, or because the task pauses while waiting for external inputs, memory management becomes more demanding than in single-session tasks.

The challenge is that context is lost between sessions. What the agent knows, what it has tried, what worked and what didn't, the reasoning behind decisions made: all of this needs to be explicitly persisted and retrieved rather than relying on the session context.

Session boundary memory management is a pattern I've found works well for this: at the end of each session, generate a structured session summary that captures the session's accomplishments, open questions, and relevant context for the next session. At the beginning of each subsequent session, retrieve the most recent session summary and use it to reconstruct the working context.

The structured session summary should be significantly more compressed than the full session history, capturing only what matters for future work. A research task session summary might include: which sources were examined, what key findings emerged, what questions remain open, what the next planned steps are. This gives the agent enough context to continue intelligently without requiring access to the full session history.

Chapter 4 Additional Content: Choosing the Right Model

Model selection is a decision that affects cost, quality, and latency. Making it thoughtfully requires understanding the specific requirements of the task, not just the general capabilities of different models.

Benchmark performance is a poor guide to model selection for specific applications. Benchmarks measure average performance across a wide range of tasks; they tell you little about performance on your specific task in your specific context.

What works better is direct empirical testing on a representative sample of your actual task. Build a test set of 50-100 representative inputs, run multiple model options on it, evaluate the outputs against your quality criteria, and measure the cost and latency. The model that produces the best quality at acceptable cost and latency for your specific task is the right choice, regardless of benchmark rankings.

For most production agentic systems, cost is a significant factor because the system makes many model calls, often including multiple calls per user request. A model that produces marginally better output at three times the cost per call might produce worse overall economics than a cheaper model with slightly lower per-output quality. Running the math on your specific expected usage volume helps make this concrete.

Chapter 5 Additional Content: Prompt Design as Engineering Discipline

Prompt design has matured enough to be called an engineering discipline, though it's still more art than science in some respects. A few principles that have held up well.

The specification principle: prompts should specify what you want, not describe what you want. There's a subtle but important difference. "Please provide a helpful and detailed response" describes a desired quality. "Respond in three sections: a direct answer, the evidence supporting it, and any important caveats" specifies a structure. Specification produces more consistent and more evaluable outputs.

The example principle: examples are often more effective than instructions for specifying desired behavior, particularly for format and style requirements. If you want outputs in a specific format, show an example rather than describing the format. The model will typically pattern-match more accurately than it will follow verbal instructions about format.

The constraint principle: negative constraints, specifying what not to do, are often as important as positive instructions. "Do not include personal opinions or recommendations unless explicitly asked" is a useful constraint for a fact-finding agent. "Do not generate code examples unless the user specifically requests them" is useful for a non-technical user agent. These constraints prevent the model from doing things that come naturally to it but aren't appropriate for the use case.

The coherence principle: all instructions in a prompt should be consistent with each other. Contradictory instructions produce inconsistent behavior, with the model sometimes following one instruction and sometimes the other. Reviewing prompts for internal consistency, asking "could any two instructions conflict?", catches many of the bugs that show up in deployed systems.

Prompt maintenance is as important as initial design. Prompts are not static; they need to be updated as the system's requirements change, as failure modes are discovered, and as the model's capabilities or behavior changes with new versions. Treating prompts as code, with version control and change documentation, is worth the overhead.

SECTION II: Architectures That Enable Autonomy

Chapter 6

The CWD Pattern: Coordinator, Worker, Delegator

I want to be careful about calling this a "pattern" in the formal sense, because I didn't derive it from first principles. I arrived at it through trial and error and recognized it as a recurring solution to recurring problems. Other teams have arrived at similar structures independently, which suggests it's capturing something real about the problem shape.

The basic problem is this: complex tasks involve subtasks that are heterogeneous in their requirements. Researching a topic requires different capabilities than writing prose, which requires different capabilities than validating facts, which requires different capabilities than formatting output. If you try to do all of this in a single agent with a single system prompt, you end up with a system that does everything reasonably and nothing particularly well. More practically, you end up with prompts that are trying to do too many things at once, which makes them brittle and hard to debug.

The CWD structure separates these concerns.

The Coordinator holds the plan. Its job is to understand the overall goal, break it into steps, track progress, and know when to revise the plan. It doesn't do the actual work, it manages the work. A good coordinator is good at decomposition and at recognizing when something has gone wrong that requires changing course.

Workers execute specific subtasks. Each worker is optimized for a narrow type of work: research, writing, validation, formatting, whatever the domain requires. Workers receive explicit, bounded instructions from the coordinator and return results. They don't need to understand the overall goal; they need to do their specific part well.

The Delegator handles routing and resource allocation. Its job is to decide which worker is best suited to a given task, manage retries and fallbacks when a worker fails, and decide when something should be escalated to a human. In simple implementations, the coordinator and delegator roles are merged; in complex ones, separating them improves clarity.

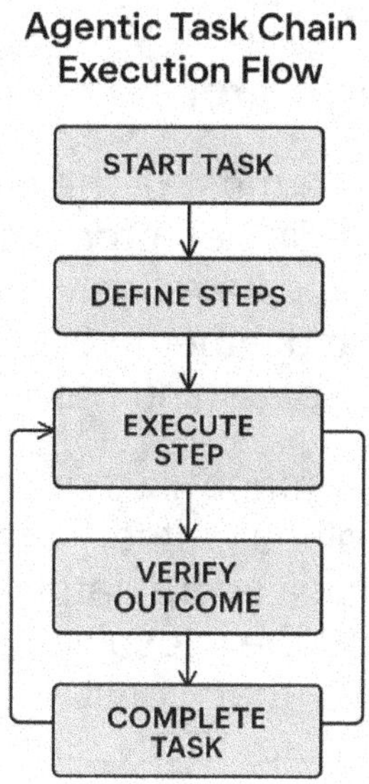

Why This Works

The separation of concerns is the main benefit. When a worker fails, you know to look at the worker, not the coordinator. When the overall plan is wrong, you know to look at the coordinator. When tasks are being routed incorrectly, you look at the delegator. This makes debugging vastly easier.

It also makes specialization possible. A research worker can have a system prompt specifically designed for retrieving and synthesizing information, with instructions tuned for that task. A writing worker can have a different prompt entirely. You're not trying to be all things at once.

The pattern scales because you can add workers for new task types without changing the coordinator or delegator. It degrades gracefully because if a worker is unavailable or fails persistently, the delegator can route to a fallback or escalate. It also supports parallelism: independent tasks can be delegated to workers simultaneously rather than running sequentially.

Designing the Coordinator

The coordinator is where most of the interesting design work happens. A weak coordinator produces plans that are too vague for workers to execute reliably, fails to recognize when a plan is not working, and either over-escalates to humans or under-escalates when something has genuinely gone wrong.

The key insight I have found is that the coordinator should produce structured plans rather than natural language descriptions. When I ask a coordinator to generate a plan as a list of prose steps, the resulting steps tend to be underspecified in ways that cause problems downstream. When I ask it to produce a JSON structure where each task has a description, expected output format, dependencies, and a success criterion, the plans are clearer and the workers have enough information to execute reliably.

This also makes the coordinator's plan machine-readable, which means you can validate it programmatically before starting execution. You can check that all dependencies are resolvable, that the expected output formats match what the downstream tasks need, and that the plan is logically coherent. Catching plan errors before execution starts is much cheaper than catching them midway through.

The coordinator also needs to be good at recognizing failure and replanning. I usually include explicit instructions about when to abandon the current plan and start over versus when to retry a failed step with a modified approach. The most useful heuristic I have found: if the same step fails twice with the same approach, try a different approach; if it fails three times overall, escalate.

Designing the Workers

Workers are where you can invest heavily in specialization. A well-designed worker for a specific task type will significantly outperform a general-purpose agent doing the same task, because its system prompt can be precisely tuned for that task without the compromises required by a broader role.

The most important principle for worker design is explicit output contracts. Each worker should know exactly what format its output should take and why. The coordinator and the workers need to agree on this format. When output formats are implicit, you end up with workers that produce plausible-looking output that the coordinator cannot actually parse or use.

Workers should also be designed to fail gracefully and informatively. When a worker cannot complete its task, it should return a structured failure response that includes what it tried, why it failed, and what information would be needed to succeed. This gives the coordinator enough to decide whether to retry, escalate, or modify the plan.

Designing the Delegator

In simple systems, the delegator is just a routing function: given a task type, which worker handles it? In more complex systems, the delegator makes more interesting decisions.

Cost-aware routing is one of the most valuable delegator behaviors. Not every task requires the most capable model. A task that involves straightforward extraction from a well-structured document can often be handled by a cheaper, faster model. A task that requires nuanced reasoning about ambiguous information needs a more capable one. Building this routing logic into the delegator, rather than always using the same model for everything, can reduce costs substantially without sacrificing quality on the tasks that matter.

Failure-aware routing is another valuable behavior. If a worker consistently fails on a specific type of task, the delegator should route those tasks to a fallback worker or flag them for human review rather than continuing to send them to a worker that cannot handle them. Tracking failure rates per worker per task type and adjusting routing accordingly is worth the implementation effort.

Some Implementation Notes

The coordinator's system prompt needs to be explicit about how it breaks down tasks. Asking it to produce a structured task graph, where each task has a description, expected output format, dependencies on other tasks, and a success criterion, works better than having it reason about the plan in natural language.

Workers should receive only what they need. Don't pass the full conversation history to a worker that only needs to summarize a document. The coordinator should extract the relevant context and pass it explicitly. This keeps costs down and reduces the noise the worker has to reason through.

Track task state explicitly. Don't rely on the coordinator to remember what's been completed. Maintain a task graph in your application logic, update it as workers complete tasks, and inject the current state into each coordinator call. This makes the system resilient to context limits and model errors.

When Not to Use This Pattern

CWD adds complexity that's not always warranted. For simple, single-step tasks, it's overkill. For tasks where the full context needs to be available at every step, the separation can actually hurt. For very quick tasks, the overhead of coordinating between components may exceed the benefit.

The right question is whether the task has natural subtasks that benefit from different optimization. If yes, CWD helps. If the task is essentially unitary, a simpler single-agent approach is probably better.

Chapter 7

Reactive Agents: The Useful Simplicity

A reactive agent does one thing: it observes an input and produces an output. No planning, no persistent state, no memory of previous interactions. Input goes in, output comes out.

This is much simpler than what I've been describing in previous chapters, and that simplicity is the point. A lot of useful applications don't require sophisticated planning or multi-step reasoning. They require reliable, fast responses to well-defined inputs.

A spam filter is a reactive agent. It looks at an email and classifies it. It doesn't need to plan; it needs to classify well. A sentiment classifier is a reactive agent. A content moderator making a first-pass decision on whether something violates policy is a reactive agent. A system that detects whether a user input is a question, a command, or something else and routes accordingly is a reactive agent.

What Makes Reactive Agents Valuable

The value of reactive agents is often underappreciated because they seem simple. But simplicity is an engineering virtue. A reactive component that reliably does one thing well is much easier to test, debug, and maintain than a complex agent that does many things adequately.

For high-volume tasks, reactive agents are often the only financially viable option. Processing a million classification requests per day with a full deliberative agent would be prohibitively expensive. The same task with a well-tuned reactive component might be orders of magnitude cheaper. The cost difference often justifies significant engineering investment in making the reactive component reliable.

Reactive agents are also inherently more predictable. Because they don't have persistent state, the same input always produces the same type of processing. This makes them easier to test thoroughly, easier to reason about in production, and easier to debug when something goes wrong.

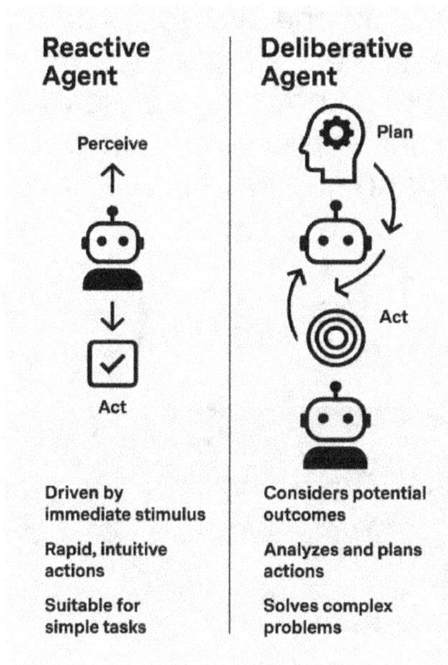

Where They Fit in Larger Systems

In complex agentic systems, reactive components often handle the outer boundary. A user sends a request; a reactive classifier determines what type of request it is and where it should go. A tool returns a result; a reactive parser extracts the relevant data. A worker produces an output; a reactive validator checks whether it meets format requirements.

One pattern I use regularly is a reactive "input classifier" at the front of complex systems. Before doing any expensive work, I run the user's input through a cheap classifier that determines what type of task it is. If it's a simple FAQ question, respond immediately from a knowledge base. If it's a task the system handles well, route to the main agent. If it's something outside the system's scope, respond with a graceful explanation rather than routing to an agent that will fail. This saves significant cost and improves the user experience substantially.

The savings from this kind of front-end classification are often larger than expected. In one system I worked on, roughly 40% of incoming requests were simple FAQ queries that could be handled directly from a knowledge base without any LLM call. Routing those to a full agentic workflow would have tripled the cost per request for no quality improvement.

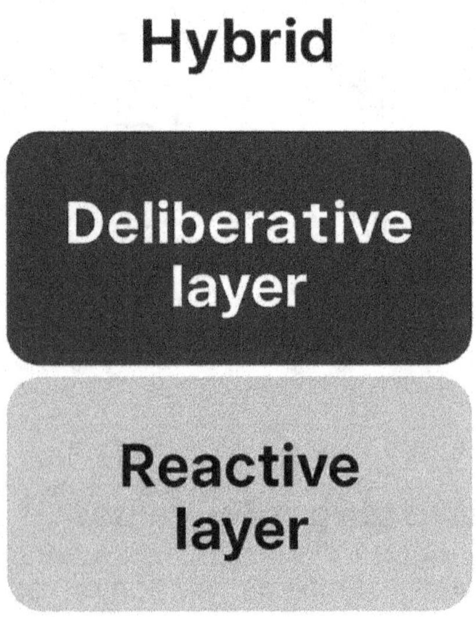

The LLM-as-Reactive-Agent Pattern

An LLM operating in a single call with no tools and no persistent state is, for practical purposes, a reactive agent. This is how most LLM-based systems are used, and while it's often appropriate for simple cases, it's worth being explicit about the limitation: a single call can't do anything that requires memory of previous interactions, can't use tools, and can't execute a multi-step plan.

The reactive LLM pattern is well-suited for: summarization, classification, extraction, reformatting, answering questions from provided context, and generating variations on a theme. It's poorly suited for: research, anything requiring tool use, anything requiring persistent memory, anything where quality depends strongly on iteration and refinement.

The confusion between "I'm using a capable LLM" and "I have an agent" is partly because reactive LLM applications work well for a wide range of tasks that feel sophisticated, even though they're architecturally simple. The limits show up when you try to extend them to tasks they're not suited for.

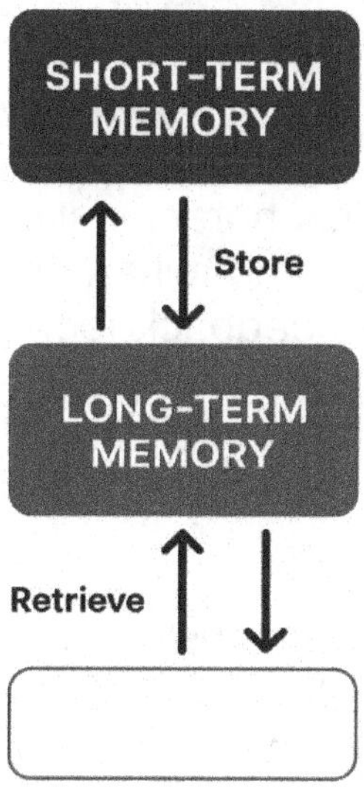

Building Reliable Reactive Components

The key to a good reactive component is precise specification. The input format should be clearly defined and validated. The output format should be equally clear, with explicit handling for edge cases. The failure behavior should be defined: what does the component return when it cannot process the input?

Testing reactive components is relatively straightforward: you can write unit tests that cover the range of expected inputs and verify the outputs. This is worth doing thoroughly, because a reactive component that fails on a common input pattern will cause problems throughout any larger system that depends on it.

I usually spend more time testing reactive components than their apparent simplicity would suggest is necessary, because they handle the high-volume common cases and a failure there affects a large fraction of requests. An agentic component that fails on 5% of complex edge cases is much less disruptive than a reactive classifier that misroutes 5% of the most common request type.

Limitations Worth Being Explicit About

Reactive agents fail in characteristic ways. They have no mechanism for recognizing when they've made an error, because they have no feedback loop. They have no way to resolve ambiguity by asking follow-up questions, unless you build that into the interface explicitly. They can't handle tasks that require gathering additional information that wasn't in the original input.

These are structural limitations, not model limitations. A more capable model won't fix them. The fix is switching to a different architecture when the task requires it. The challenge is recognizing when that switch is warranted.

Chapter 8

Deliberative Agents: Planning, Search, and Reflection

A deliberative agent thinks before it acts. Rather than mapping directly from input to output, it maintains an internal model of the situation, reasons about possible actions, and chooses based on anticipated outcomes. This is slower and more expensive than reactive behavior, but it's necessary for tasks where the right action depends on understanding context that isn't immediately obvious.

Planning

Planning, in this context, means generating a sequence of actions that will achieve a goal, taking into account dependencies between actions and the likelihood that each step will succeed.

The most common planning approach with language models is to have the planner generate a task breakdown in a structured format, then execute each step in sequence. This works well for many cases, but it has a fundamental limitation: the plan is generated upfront before the agent has gathered any information, so it's based entirely on what the model knew at planning time. For tasks where the details matter a lot, a plan that can't be revised in light of new information is fragile.

Better practice is adaptive planning: generate an initial plan, but treat it as a hypothesis rather than a commitment. After each step, the agent evaluates whether the plan is still appropriate given what was learned and revises if needed. This adds overhead but significantly improves reliability for complex tasks.

The planning prompt matters a lot. Explicitly asking the model to identify potential failure modes for each step, and to specify what "done" looks like for each step, produces much better plans than asking it to just list the steps. Building in uncertainty, asking "which of these steps is most likely to fail, and what would you do if it did?", produces plans that are more realistic about the task.

I have also found it useful to have the planner estimate confidence for each step. When the planner flags a step as low-confidence, that is a signal to either gather more information before attempting it or to involve a human. High-confidence steps can often proceed automatically. This simple heuristic, treating the planner's own confidence estimates as an input to the execution strategy, improves system reliability without requiring sophisticated uncertainty quantification.

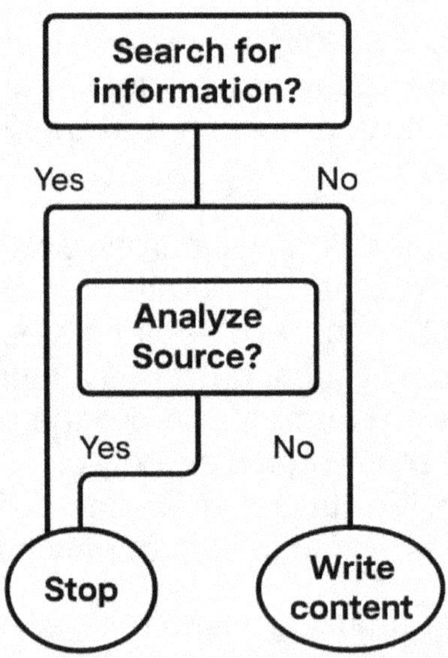

Search

Search here means exploring a space of possible actions or strategies to find the best one, rather than committing immediately to the first thing that comes to mind.

For agentic systems, the most practical form of search is what's sometimes called Tree of Thought: the agent generates multiple candidate next steps, evaluates each one, and pursues the most promising. This is slower than simply generating the next step, but for tasks where the right direction isn't obvious, the quality improvement is worth it.

Tree of Thought works well for tasks like debugging (generate multiple hypotheses about what's wrong, evaluate each), creative tasks (generate multiple approaches, evaluate which is strongest), and planning (generate multiple plan variants, choose the best). It's overkill for tasks with obvious next steps.

The evaluation step is where this can get expensive. Evaluating a candidate action might require trying it (expensive, and some actions have side effects) or having the model reason about it (cheaper but less reliable). In practice, I use a two-stage approach: cheap model evaluation first to eliminate clearly bad options, then more thorough evaluation of the remaining candidates.

Reflection

Reflection is an agent reviewing its own outputs and reasoning. This is surprisingly useful, partly because the model often catches errors in its own outputs when given the explicit task of reviewing them, and partly because the reflection process itself can surface important considerations that were missed in the initial pass.

The simplest version is asking the model to review its output before returning it. This adds one model call to the cost but often produces meaningfully better outputs, particularly for tasks where correctness matters.

More sophisticated reflection involves having the model assess its own confidence, identify the assumptions underlying its reasoning, and flag where those assumptions might be wrong. This produces outputs that are more honest about their limitations, which is valuable in contexts where the user needs to know how much to trust the result.

One pattern I use for research tasks: after the agent has gathered information and drafted a response, I have it run a "skeptic pass", reviewing the response as if looking for reasons it might be wrong. This catches overconfident claims and unfounded generalizations that the initial generation missed.

The Tradeoff with Reactive Approaches

Deliberative approaches are better for: tasks where the right approach isn't obvious, tasks where errors are costly and hard to reverse, tasks requiring multi-step reasoning, tasks where quality matters more than speed.

Reactive approaches are better for: high-volume low-stakes decisions, tasks with well-defined inputs and outputs, latency-sensitive applications, situations where the deliberative overhead would exceed the value.

In practice, most sophisticated systems use both. Building the routing logic to decide which path to take is itself a design challenge, but it's usually worth the effort.

Chapter 9

Hybrid Architectures: Combining Fast and Slow

The most reliable agentic systems I've worked with don't choose between reactive and deliberative behavior. They use both, with logic that routes between them based on the characteristics of the task at hand.

This isn't a novel insight. Daniel Kahneman's description of System 1 (fast, intuitive, automatic) and System 2 (slow, deliberate, effortful) thinking describes the same structure in human cognition. The analogy is imperfect but useful: just as humans rely on automatic responses for familiar situations and deliberate reasoning for novel or high-stakes ones, well-designed agents should use fast reactive processing where it's sufficient and slow deliberative processing where it's necessary.

The Routing Problem

The central design challenge in hybrid architectures is the routing logic: given an input, how do you decide whether it requires reactive or deliberative handling?

Simple approaches work surprisingly well. You can route based on task type, confidence level, stakes, or complexity. The challenge is that these dimensions can conflict. A high-stakes but simple task might be served well by a reliable, fast reactive system. A low-stakes but complex task might not warrant the cost of deliberative processing.

My general approach is to start with deliberative handling for all cases, identify the subcases where reactive handling is reliable enough, and gradually shift those to the reactive path as confidence builds. This is more conservative than necessary but avoids the costly mistakes that come from over-optimizing for speed early.

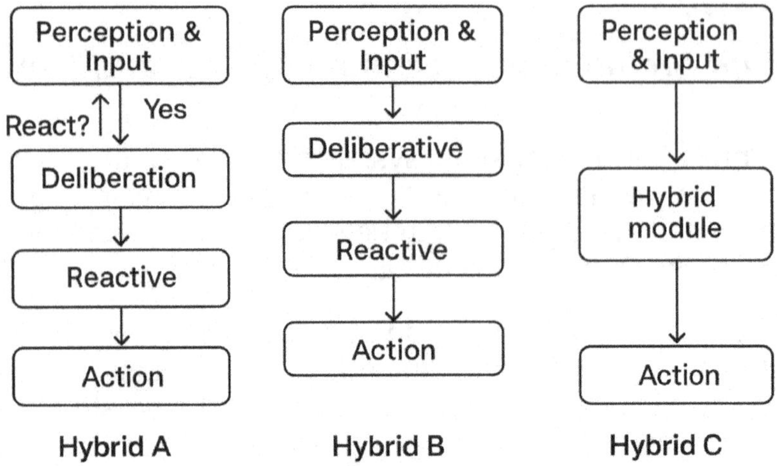

Hybrid Architectures

Embedding Reactive Checks in Deliberative Flows

One pattern that comes up often is using reactive components at specific points in a deliberative workflow, rather than choosing between them at the routing stage.

A deliberative research agent generates a plan, retrieves information, and synthesizes a report. Embedded in this workflow, at the retrieval step, there's a reactive classifier that checks whether each retrieved document is actually relevant to the question before passing it to the synthesis step. This prevents the slow, expensive synthesis step from wasting effort on irrelevant material.

Similarly: a deliberative content generation agent produces a draft. Before the draft is returned to the user, a reactive content moderator checks it against policy. If it passes, it's returned directly. If it fails, it's sent back for revision. This adds minimal latency for the common case while handling the uncommon case appropriately.

State Management Across the Hybrid

The trickier design challenge is state management when reactive and deliberative components share state.

A reactive component that's part of a deliberative workflow needs to read from and sometimes write to shared state. Treating shared state as a first-class concern, designing the state representation carefully, being explicit about what each component reads and writes, and building in consistency checks saves an enormous amount of debugging time.

Practical Calibration

Getting the reactive/deliberative boundary right is an iterative process. You observe the system in operation, identify where reactive handling is failing and where deliberative handling is being used unnecessarily, adjust the routing thresholds, and repeat.

Track escalation rate explicitly: how often does the system decide that neither path is appropriate and it needs human involvement? If this rate is too high, the system isn't working. If it's too low, the system may be trying to handle things it shouldn't. A calibrated escalation rate, appropriate for the stakes of the use case, is a sign that the routing logic is working.

Chapter 6 Additional Content: CWD in Practice

Building the Coordinator Prompt

The coordinator prompt is one of the most important documents you'll write for a CWD system, and it requires more care than most prompts because small changes in how the coordinator reasons about decomposition can have large effects on downstream quality.

I've settled on a template structure for coordinator prompts that works well across different domains. The template has five sections: role definition, goal format, task decomposition instructions, output format specification, and failure handling instructions.

The role definition describes what the coordinator is and is not responsible for. "You are responsible for breaking complex goals into specific, executable tasks and tracking their completion. You are not responsible for executing tasks yourself, assessing the quality of task outputs beyond verifying format compliance, or making domain-specific judgments. Those responsibilities belong to specialized workers."

The goal format section specifies exactly how goals will be presented to the coordinator and what fields it can rely on. Clear goal format specification prevents the coordinator from making assumptions about information that may or may not be present.

The task decomposition instructions are where most of the behavioral engineering happens. The most important instruction I've found: "Before generating tasks, identify the dependencies between them. A task that depends on the output of another task cannot begin until that task is complete. Identify these dependencies explicitly in your output."

The output format specification requires the coordinator to produce tasks as structured JSON rather than prose. Structured output is machine-readable, can be validated before execution begins, and forces the coordinator to be specific about things like expected output format and success criteria.

The failure handling instructions tell the coordinator what to do when a worker fails: "If a worker reports a failure, evaluate whether the failure can be resolved by retrying with different parameters, requires routing to a different worker, requires revising the plan, or requires escalation to a human. Return a structured decision with your reasoning."

Real-World CWD Variations

The basic CWD pattern adapts to many different domains, but the adaptations are more significant than they might seem. Here are a few variations worth understanding.

The pipeline CWD processes tasks in a fixed sequence: coordinator assigns step 1 to worker 1, coordinator receives output and assigns step 2 to worker 2, and so on. This is appropriate when tasks have strict dependencies and parallel execution isn't possible. The advantage is simplicity and predictability. The disadvantage is that it's slow for complex tasks and a failure in any step blocks everything downstream.

The parallel CWD coordinates workers executing independent tasks simultaneously. The coordinator identifies which tasks can be executed in parallel, issues all of them at once, and waits for all to complete before synthesizing the results. This is faster but requires careful design to ensure that parallel tasks are actually independent and that the synthesis step handles partial failures.

The recursive CWD allows worker agents to themselves be coordinators for sub-tasks. A high-level coordinator decomposes a complex goal and assigns major components to workers, each of which then coordinates its own set of lower-level workers. This is appropriate for very complex tasks with hierarchical structure. The risk is complexity: debugging recursive coordinator-worker systems requires tracing through multiple levels of decomposition.

The adaptive CWD revises its plan during execution based on what workers report. Rather than executing a fixed plan from start to finish, the coordinator evaluates after each step whether the plan is still appropriate and revises if needed. This adds overhead but handles cases where early results reveal that the original plan was wrong.

Testing CWD Systems

Testing CWD systems is more complex than testing single-agent systems because you're testing not just the behavior of individual components but the coordination between them.

Worker testing in isolation: before testing the full system, test each worker independently with controlled inputs. Define the range of inputs each worker should handle, write test cases covering that range, and verify that the worker's outputs match expected formats and quality. This baseline testing catches worker-level problems before they become harder-to-diagnose coordination problems.

Coordinator testing with mock workers: test the coordinator's decomposition and routing behavior by replacing real workers with mock implementations that return controlled outputs. This lets you test coordinator logic without the variability of real worker outputs. Verify that the coordinator produces reasonable task decompositions for a range of goal types, routes tasks to appropriate workers, and handles failures as expected.

Integration testing with failure injection: test the full system with deliberate failures injected at different points. What happens when worker 2 fails after workers 1 and 3 have already succeeded? Does the coordinator retry, revise the plan, or escalate? Does it produce a meaningful error message? These edge cases are where most production failures occur.

Monitoring CWD Systems in Production

The metrics I find most useful for monitoring CWD systems in production:

Task completion rate by worker: if one worker is completing tasks at a lower rate than others, it's a signal that either its task load is wrong (it's receiving tasks it can't handle) or its prompt needs updating.

Plan revision rate: how often is the coordinator revising its plan during execution? A high revision rate might indicate that initial planning is poor, or it might indicate that the coordinator is appropriately adaptive. Distinguishing these requires looking at whether revisions improve or hurt final output quality.

Delegation depth: in recursive CWD systems, how many levels of delegation are tasks going through? Very deep delegation chains are often a sign that the coordinator is over-decomposing tasks, which increases latency and cost without necessarily improving quality.

Time in coordinator vs. time in workers: if the system is slow, is the bottleneck in coordinator planning or in worker execution? These suggest different interventions.

Chapter 7 Additional Content: Reactive Architecture Patterns

Reactive Chains

Multiple reactive agents can be composed in chains where the output of one becomes the input of the next. This pattern is simple and powerful: each agent in the chain does one thing well, and the chain as a whole accomplishes something more complex.

A content processing chain might look like: input validator (checks that input meets format requirements), content classifier (determines content type and appropriate processing path), transformer (converts content to the required output format), quality checker (verifies output meets quality criteria), output router (sends output to appropriate destination).

Each component in this chain is a simple reactive agent. The chain as a whole handles a complex workflow. The advantage is that each component can be tested independently, replaced when better approaches become available, and debugged in isolation when something goes wrong.

The main design challenge with reactive chains is that errors at one step affect all subsequent steps. A good practice is to build validation checks between each pair of components: before component N+1 starts processing, verify that component N's output actually meets the input requirements for component N+1. This catches format errors early and produces clearer error messages.

Stateful Reactive Agents

Calling an agent "reactive" does not mean it can't have state at all. It means the state is bounded and well-defined rather than accumulating indefinitely.

A rate limiter is a stateful reactive agent: it maintains a count of recent requests and applies rate limiting rules based on that count. Its state is bounded (it only tracks recent history) and its decision logic is reactive (each request triggers a decision based on current state). This is a different kind of state than a deliberative agent's evolving goal representation.

Bounded-state reactive agents are useful for: rate limiting and throttling, session tracking (is this request part of an ongoing session or a new one?), simple personalization (apply this user's stored preferences), and caching (has this request been seen before, and can the cached result be returned?).

The key design principle: reactive agent state should be small, well-defined, and queryable. If you can't describe exactly what state the agent maintains and how it updates, the agent is probably not truly reactive and should be designed as deliberative instead.

Chapter 8 Additional Content: Deliberative Planning Patterns

Chain-of-Thought in Practice

Chain-of-thought prompting is one of the highest-return techniques in the deliberative agent toolkit, and the practical implementation details matter more than the concept suggests.

The basic version: add "Let me think through this step by step" or equivalent to the prompt, and the model will generate reasoning before generating the final answer. This works because it forces the model to work through the problem rather than jumping to an answer, and the generated reasoning provides a check you can inspect before using the final answer.

The failure mode to watch for: the model sometimes generates reasoning that looks correct but leads to a wrong answer, or generates reasoning that justifies a pre-chosen answer rather than working toward it. This is called "post-hoc rationalization" and it's a genuine problem. One mitigation: ask the model to generate multiple independent chains of thought and compare them. If they all lead to the same answer, confidence is higher. If they diverge, that's a signal for human review.

Self-consistency sampling is a more rigorous approach: generate multiple completions with non-zero temperature (so they're different), and take the majority vote as the answer. For factual questions, this significantly reduces hallucination compared to single-sample generation. For reasoning tasks, it improves reliability at the cost of multiple model calls.

Hierarchical Planning

For complex tasks, a single-level plan is often not detailed enough to execute reliably. Hierarchical planning breaks the task into levels of abstraction: a high-level plan that specifies what to accomplish, a mid-level plan that specifies how to accomplish each high-level step, and an execution-level plan that specifies the specific actions to take.

The advantage of hierarchical planning is that it allows high-level reasoning about the overall approach (should we tackle this problem from direction A or direction B?) to be separated from low-level reasoning about execution details (which specific API call implements this step?). Mixing these concerns in a single plan tends to produce plans that are incoherent at one level or the other.

The implementation: generate the high-level plan first and validate it with a human or a separate evaluation step. Then, for each high-level step, generate the mid-level plan and validate it. Then execute the mid-level plan. This staged approach adds overhead but catches plan problems at the appropriate level of abstraction rather than discovering them during execution.

Chapter 9 Additional Content: Hybrid Architecture Implementation

Confidence-Based Routing Implementation

Implementing reliable confidence-based routing is harder than it sounds, because language models are poorly calibrated: they tend to be overconfident, reporting high confidence even when they're wrong.

Several approaches have been developed to improve calibration. Temperature scaling adjusts the model's confidence scores after the fact based on observed accuracy in a calibration set. This requires having a calibration dataset, which requires deploying the system and collecting labeled outputs. It's the most principled approach but requires production data.

Ensemble methods use multiple model calls and compare the results. If three independent calls all agree on the answer, confidence is higher than if they disagree. This is expensive (three times as many calls) but doesn't require calibration data.

Verbalized confidence is asking the model to express its confidence as text ("I'm highly confident this is X" versus "I'm not certain but I think this might be Y") rather than relying on implicit confidence from the token probabilities. Verbalized confidence is less reliable than calibrated numeric scores but is better than nothing and requires no additional infrastructure.

The practical recommendation: start with verbalized confidence (it's cheap and easy), monitor the relationship between expressed confidence and actual accuracy, and invest in proper calibration if you deploy at significant scale.

Hybrid System Observability

Hybrid systems are harder to observe than pure reactive or pure deliberative systems because you need visibility into both the routing decisions and the behavior of each path.

The key metrics to track: what fraction of requests are routed to the reactive path versus the deliberative path? Of reactive-path requests, what fraction are handled correctly? Of deliberative-path requests, what fraction are handled correctly? How do these rates change over time?

If the reactive path's accuracy is degrading over time, either the reactive classifier needs updating (the distribution of inputs has shifted) or the reactive agents themselves need updating. If the deliberative path is handling too many simple cases, the routing threshold is set wrong. These are different problems with different solutions.

Instrumenting the routing decision separately from the downstream behavior is important: you want to be able to analyze routing decisions in isolation without having to look at the full request and response.

Chapter 6 Extended: Building CWD Systems with LangGraph and CrewAI

The CWD pattern is abstract enough that it can be implemented in many different ways. In practice, most teams building these systems today use either LangGraph or CrewAI, and the two frameworks make different tradeoffs worth understanding.

LangGraph approaches coordination as a state graph. You define nodes (which can be language model calls, tool calls, or custom Python functions) and edges (which define the flow of control between nodes, possibly with conditional branching). State flows through the graph as a typed object that each node can read from and write to. This gives you very explicit control over the coordination logic and makes the flow of execution easy to trace and debug.

A CWD system in LangGraph has a coordinator node that generates the plan, a delegator node that routes tasks to worker subgraphs, and worker subgraphs that each implement a specific task type. The shared state object holds the plan, the status of each task, and the accumulated outputs. Each node reads what it needs from state and writes its outputs back.

The advantage of the LangGraph approach: explicit state management, easy observability, and the ability to implement complex conditional logic in code rather than trying to express it in prompts. The disadvantage: more boilerplate to write and a steeper learning curve if you're not familiar with graph-based programming.

CrewAI approaches coordination through role-based agents and tasks. You define agents with roles, goals, and backstories; define tasks with descriptions, expected outputs, and assigned agents; and configure a crew with a process type (sequential, hierarchical, or custom). CrewAI handles the coordination logic automatically based on the process configuration.

A CWD system in CrewAI defines a Coordinator agent, a Delegator agent, and multiple Worker agents. The task list describes what needs to be done, and CrewAI's hierarchical process manages the flow of work between agents. The shared context between agents is managed by CrewAI's memory system.

The advantage of the CrewAI approach: less boilerplate, faster to get a working prototype, and good built-in support for multi-agent collaboration patterns. The disadvantage: less explicit control over coordination logic, which can make complex branching or custom failure handling harder to implement.

For most production use cases I've worked with, LangGraph is better for systems that need complex conditional logic, custom state management, or tight integration with existing infrastructure. CrewAI is better for getting a proof of concept running quickly and for systems where the standard coordination patterns fit the use case well.

LangGraph Implementation Pattern

Here's the skeleton of a CWD implementation in LangGraph that illustrates the key patterns:

The state object holds: the original goal, the current plan (a list of task objects), the status of each task, the outputs produced by workers, and any errors encountered. Every node in the graph reads from and writes to this state object.

The coordinator node generates the plan: it receives the goal from state, uses a language model to decompose it into tasks with explicit dependencies and success criteria, and writes the plan back to state. It also writes an initial assessment of which tasks can be executed in parallel.

The delegator node is called after the coordinator and after each worker completes. It reads the current plan status from state and decides what to do next: identify tasks whose dependencies are all complete and route them to the appropriate worker, check whether the plan needs revision based on worker outputs, or determine that all tasks are complete and the goal is achieved.

Worker nodes each implement a specific task type. They read the task assigned to them from state, execute it (which might involve tool calls, further model calls, or custom Python logic), and write their output and status back to state.

The graph connects these nodes with conditional edges: after the coordinator, go to the delegator; after the delegator, go to the appropriate worker or to a completion node; after each worker, go back to the delegator.

CrewAI Implementation Pattern

A CrewAI implementation of the same pattern looks different but achieves similar results. You define the coordinator, delegator, and worker agents with their roles and tools. You define the task types as Task objects with descriptions and expected output formats. The Crew object is configured with a hierarchical process, which means the coordinator agent manages the delegation to other agents.

The key difference is that CrewAI's hierarchical process handles the task routing logic automatically. You don't write explicit routing code; instead, the coordinator agent decides how to delegate based on its role description and the task descriptions. This is simpler but gives you less control over exactly how routing decisions are made.

Testing CWD with LangGraph vs CrewAI

Testing strategies also differ between the two frameworks. LangGraph's explicit state makes it straightforward to inject test state and verify that each node transforms it correctly. You can unit test nodes in isolation by constructing a specific state object and verifying the output.

CrewAI is more opaque about its internal state, which makes unit testing harder. Integration testing, running the full crew on test inputs and verifying outputs, is the more natural approach. The tradeoff is that integration tests take longer to run and failures are harder to diagnose.

Chapter 7 Extended: Reactive Agent Performance and Scaling

Scaling Reactive Components

Reactive agents have a significant advantage over deliberative agents for scaling: because they're stateless and each request is independent, they parallelize trivially. You can run many instances of a reactive component simultaneously without any coordination overhead.

This makes reactive components suitable for high-throughput workloads that would be impractical for deliberative agents. A content moderation system that needs to review millions of posts per day requires reactive architecture; a deliberative system that carefully reasons about each post would be too slow and expensive at that volume.

Optimizing reactive components for throughput requires attention to latency at every layer: model call latency, parsing and validation latency, and any I/O latency (database lookups, cache checks). For high-volume workloads, even small improvements in latency per request compound to large throughput improvements.

Batching is one of the highest-leverage techniques for reactive component performance. Rather than making one model call per input, batch multiple inputs into a single call and extract multiple outputs. Most model providers support batch inference, and the efficiency gain can be substantial for high-volume use cases.

Caching is complementary to batching. If many requests have identical or near-identical inputs, returning cached results is much faster than making a model call. The challenge is cache key design: for exact-match caching, the key is the full input. For semantic caching, you need to compute embeddings and do similarity lookups, which adds its own latency.

Monitoring Reactive Component Quality Over Time

Reactive components can drift in quality over time even without explicit changes, because the distribution of inputs they receive changes. A classifier trained and prompted for one distribution of inputs may behave differently as users' behavior patterns change.

Setting up a continuous evaluation pipeline for reactive components, running the component on a fixed test set periodically and tracking metric trends, catches quality drift before users notice. The test set should include recent examples collected from production, not just the examples from initial development.

A/B testing framework integration is valuable for reactive components: when you update a classifier or other reactive component, routing a fraction of traffic to the new version while monitoring quality allows you to validate the update before full rollout.

Chapter 8 Extended: Advanced Reflection Patterns

Meta-Cognitive Reflection

Beyond reflecting on the content of its outputs, an agent can reflect on its own reasoning process: did it approach this problem correctly? Is there a better way to think about this class of problem?

Meta-cognitive reflection is more expensive than object-level reflection but can produce insights that improve performance on entire classes of tasks rather than just the current instance. The pattern: after completing a task, ask the agent to reflect not just on the output but on the approach taken. What worked well? What would it do differently? What would make this class of task easier to handle?

These reflections can be stored in procedural memory and retrieved when similar tasks are encountered, gradually building up a set of heuristics for how to approach different problem types.

Reflection as Quality Control

Reflection can be structured as a quality control step rather than as open-ended self-assessment. Rather than asking "how could this be better?" you ask the agent to check the output against specific quality criteria.

Checklists are particularly effective for this. A research task might have a checklist: did you check at least three sources? Did you verify any numerical claims? Did you note any significant counterarguments? Running through this checklist as a reflection step catches common quality issues in a systematic way.

The advantage of checklist-based reflection over open-ended reflection is predictability: you know exactly what's being checked. The disadvantage is that the checklist only catches the issues you anticipated; open-ended reflection can catch unanticipated problems.

Chapter 9 Extended: Hybrid Architecture Case Examples

E-commerce Search and Recommendation

An e-commerce search and recommendation system illustrates the hybrid pattern well. The majority of queries, product searches and standard filtering, can be handled reactively: parse the query, generate an embedding, retrieve similar products, apply filters, return results. This path is fast, cheap, and highly reliable.

A minority of queries require deliberative handling: ambiguous queries that could mean several different things, complex requirements that need decomposition ("find me a gift for my grandmother who likes gardening but has limited mobility and a budget of $50"), or queries that require understanding context from earlier in the session.

The routing logic classifies queries based on complexity and ambiguity. Unambiguous, simple queries go to the reactive path. Complex or ambiguous queries go to the deliberative path, which clarifies the intent, decomposes the requirements, and assembles a more curated result set.

The practical result: the system handles 85% of queries on the reactive path with sub-100ms latency and the other 15% on the deliberative path with 500-1000ms latency. Users experience fast responses for simple queries and more thoughtful responses for complex ones.

Legal Document Processing

A legal document processing system provides another example. Documents arrive in many formats and with many different purposes. The reactive front end classifies each document by type (contract, brief, filing, correspondence) and routes it to the appropriate processing pipeline.

For standard document types, a deliberative pipeline handles extraction and analysis: extract the relevant clauses, identify the parties, summarize the key terms, flag unusual provisions. For unusual or complex documents, a more intensive deliberative process involving multiple specialized agents handles the analysis.

The classifier at the front is highly reliable for common document types, which represent most of the volume, and conservatively escalates to human review for documents it's uncertain about. The deliberative pipelines for standard types are well-optimized for their specific document type. The intensive deliberative process handles the long tail of unusual cases.

This architecture handles high document volumes efficiently while maintaining quality on complex cases, which a purely reactive or purely deliberative system couldn't achieve.

Chapter 10

Tool Use and Action Interfaces

Building a system that can use tools, really use them, reliably, in the context of a complex task, turns out to be harder than it looks from the outside. The demos make it seem straightforward: the model decides to call a function, the function returns a result, the model incorporates the result. In practice, there are failure modes at every step that you need to explicitly handle.

This chapter covers the practical side of tool integration: how to define tools well, how to handle the ways tool use fails, and how to think about the action space your agent operates in.

Defining Tools Well

The first problem is that tool descriptions need to be good enough for the model to know when and how to use them. Most APIs are designed for human developers who can read documentation, ask questions, and try things. A language model calling an API from a description in its context doesn't have those options. It has to work from whatever you put in the tool definition.

Good tool definitions are specific about what the tool does, when to use it, what the inputs mean, and what the outputs look like. They include examples. They explicitly mention what the tool is not for, or what happens in edge cases.

Vague tool descriptions lead to the model calling tools inappropriately, using a web search tool when it should be querying an internal database, or calling them with malformed inputs. The model is trying to infer intent from your description; the better the description, the more reliable the behavior.

I recommend writing tool descriptions as if they're going to be used by a very literal, very capable junior developer who has no context about your system beyond what you tell them explicitly. If that description would leave them confused about what to do in some scenario, it'll leave the model confused too.

One thing I've started doing is including negative examples in tool descriptions. Not just "this tool searches the internal knowledge base" but also "do not use this tool for current events or information that changes frequently, use the web search tool for those." This kind of negative specification catches cases where the model might reasonably infer the wrong tool is appropriate.

Tool versioning is another thing that comes up more than you'd expect. When you update a tool's behavior or interface, you need to update its description. If the description says the tool returns a list of results but you've changed it to return a paginated response object, the model will fail in confusing ways because it's trying to use the output according to the old description. Keeping tool descriptions synchronized with tool implementations is an operational practice that requires deliberate attention.

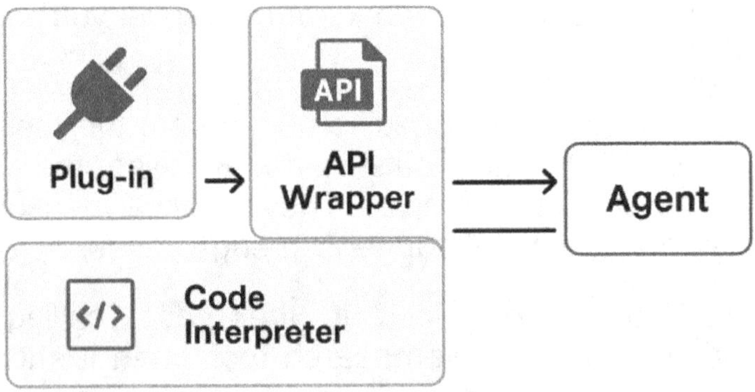

The Parsing Problem

A language model generates text. For tool use, you need it to generate text in a specific format that your code can parse and act on. OpenAI's function calling API and similar features from other providers help with this by constraining the output format, but they don't eliminate parsing failures.

The model might generate a tool call with a missing required field. It might generate a value in the wrong type. It might generate a tool call with plausible-sounding but incorrect parameter values that satisfy the schema but don't make sense semantically.

Validation at every layer helps: schema validation to catch type errors, semantic validation to catch nonsensical values, and in some cases having a separate model call review the proposed tool call before executing it. The overhead is worth it for tools with expensive or irreversible effects.

Retry and fallback logic is important. When a tool call fails, the agent needs to know what to do. Simply failing is rarely the right answer. Retry with better-formed parameters? Try a different tool? Ask the user for clarification? Escalate to a human? The right answer depends on the situation, and having explicit logic for each type of failure is better than a generic retry mechanism.

I've found it useful to classify failure types rather than handling all failures the same way. A tool call that fails because of a malformed parameter is different from one that fails because the tool itself errored, which is different from one that succeeds but returns empty results. Each type suggests a different response: fix the parameter and retry, handle the tool error, search elsewhere for the information.

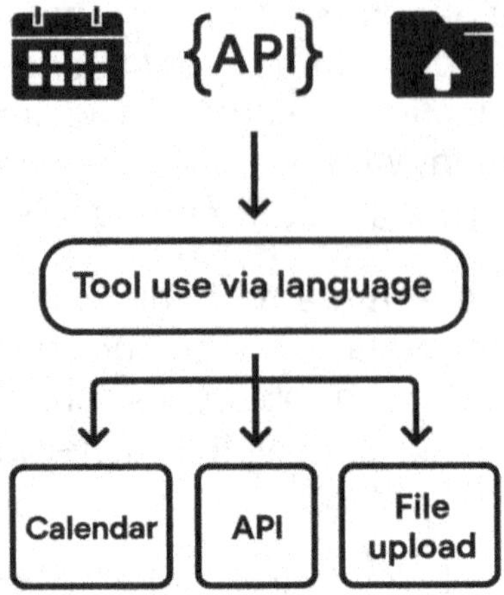

Real Complexity in Action Spaces

The action space of a real agentic system can be surprisingly large and complex, and managing it well requires thought.

Some actions are read-only: retrieve information, generate content, evaluate options. These are safe to take without much caution. If they fail, you try again. If they succeed with a poor result, you can discard the result.

Some actions have side effects that can be undone: send a draft email to a staging inbox, create a record in a database with a "pending" flag, write a file to a temp directory. These are safer than fully irreversible actions but still require care.

Some actions are irreversible: send an email for real, publish content publicly, make a financial transaction. These require explicit human approval or very high-confidence automation.

Most production agentic systems I've seen underinvest in thinking about action reversibility. The common failure mode is an agent that's been given tools that can take irreversible actions and is trusted to use them based on its own judgment, without explicit checks. This works until it doesn't, and when it doesn't, the consequences can be significant.

The right approach is to categorize every tool in your action space by its reversibility profile and build explicit handling for each category. Read-only tools need minimal protection. Side-effecting but reversible tools need logging and confirmation for significant actions. Irreversible tools need explicit human approval except for actions that meet strict criteria for automation.

Building a clear reversibility taxonomy at the start of a project, before you have built most of the tools, is worth the effort. It forces you to think carefully about what each tool actually does and to make deliberate decisions about the level of oversight required for each category. These decisions are much harder to change after you have deployed a system and users are depending on it.

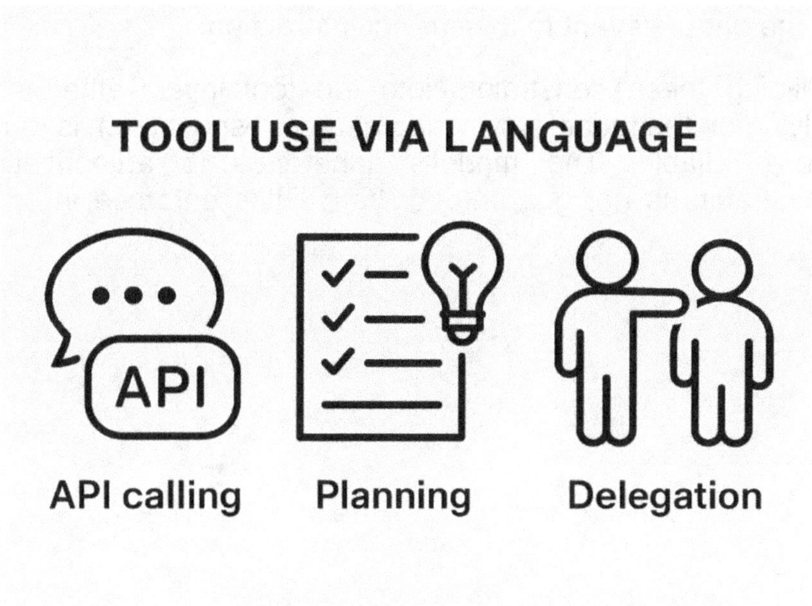

Tool Authentication and Authorization

In most real agentic systems, tools don't just need to be called correctly; they need to be called with the right credentials and with appropriate authorization for the current user and context.

Managing credentials for tools is a security concern that requires careful architecture. The agent itself should not hold credentials in its prompt context, where they might be exposed in logs or outputs. Credentials should be injected at the tool execution layer from a secure store, scoped to what the current operation actually requires.

Authorization is a separate concern from authentication. Even if the agent has credentials to call a tool, the question of whether it should call that tool in the current context is an application-level decision. An agent that can read any customer's account data in principle should not be able to read any customer's data in practice; it should be constrained to the data relevant to the current interaction.

Building these constraints into the tool layer rather than relying on the model's own judgment to respect them is much more reliable. The model's adherence to authorization constraints is not guaranteed; hard limits enforced in code are.

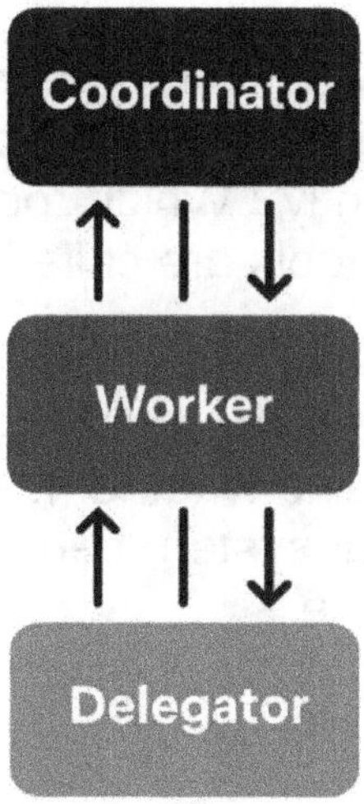

The Multi-Tool Coordination Problem

When an agent has access to multiple tools, a new problem emerges: tool selection and sequencing. Which tool should be used for this part of the task? In what order? How do the outputs of one tool inform the use of another?

For simple cases, you can let the model figure this out based on tool descriptions. For complex cases, you may want to provide explicit orchestration logic. This orchestration logic can live in the system prompt, but for complex scenarios it often works better as actual code, a pipeline that calls specific tools in a defined order, with branching based on the outputs.

One useful principle: if you find yourself spending a lot of time writing system prompt instructions about how to use tools in combination, that's a signal that the combination logic should probably be code rather than instructions.

Monitoring Tool Use in Production

Once a system is deployed, understanding how it's using tools is important for both debugging and optimization. Which tools are called most frequently? Which tools fail most often? Are there patterns in when tools are called inappropriately?

Building observability into tool use from the start saves significant time later. Log every tool call with its parameters, the result, the latency, and whether it succeeded. These logs will tell you things about system behavior that are not visible from model outputs alone.

Chapter 11

Memory and Persistence

I covered the conceptual framework for memory in Chapter 3. This chapter gets into the practical implementation: the actual systems you'll use, the tradeoffs you'll need to make, and the failure modes you need to plan for.

The Memory Stack

A production agentic system typically has several layers of memory operating simultaneously.

At the bottom, there's the context window, whatever the current model call can see. Fast, reliable, expensive to fill with irrelevant content. This is working memory: what the agent is actively thinking about right now.

Above that, there's session memory, information that persists across calls within a session but doesn't necessarily persist across sessions. Conversation history, retrieved documents from earlier in the task, intermediate results. Usually stored in memory on your application server or in a fast key-value store like Redis.

Above that, there's long-term memory, information that persists across sessions. User preferences, past interaction history, domain knowledge, learned strategies. Usually stored in a vector database for semantic retrieval, or in a structured database for precise queries. This is where most of the interesting design happens.

The interactions between these layers matter. Information flows up (things learned in this session get stored for the long term) and down (long-term memory is retrieved into the session context). Getting these flows right is as important as getting the individual layers right.

Vector Databases

Vector databases store embeddings, high-dimensional numerical representations of text, and support similarity search. This is the right tool for retrieving information based on meaning rather than exact keywords.

The main options you'll encounter: Pinecone (managed, easy to set up, somewhat expensive at scale), Weaviate (more complex to operate, better customization), Chroma (simple, good for development and smaller-scale production), FAISS (fast library, not a managed service, requires more engineering). For most cases, start with Chroma for development and Pinecone for production unless you have specific reasons to prefer something else.

The quality of what you embed matters enormously. Embedding whole documents produces retrievals that are topically relevant but may miss specific details. Chunking documents into smaller pieces before embedding gets you more precise retrieval but requires you to figure out how to chunk appropriately. Splitting mid-sentence loses context; splitting at section boundaries may produce chunks that are too large for the context window.

A practical approach that works well for most cases: chunk at paragraph boundaries, with some overlap between adjacent chunks so that information near boundaries isn't lost. The overlap means some content is duplicated in your index, but the quality improvement in retrieval is usually worth the storage cost.

Metadata filtering is underutilized. If you store metadata alongside your embeddings, source, date, type, author, you can filter the semantic search by metadata to narrow the results. This is particularly valuable when you have documents from multiple sources with different trust levels or time relevance.

Evaluation of retrieval quality is something a lot of teams skip and then regret. Building a small evaluation set, questions you know the answers to, where you can check whether the retrieval returns the information needed to answer correctly, catches degradation early and guides tuning decisions.

Retrieval quality can degrade over time as your index grows, as your query patterns change, or as the underlying documents become outdated. Setting up a regular evaluation run against a fixed test set will tell you when something has gone wrong before users notice.

Structured Storage

Not everything should go in a vector database. Structured information, user profiles, task states, explicit facts, configurations, often retrieves better from a traditional database with precise queries.

A user preference like "prefers responses under 200 words" is better stored as a structured attribute and retrieved by user ID than embedded in a vector space and retrieved by similarity. An account balance is better stored in a database with transactional guarantees than in a vector store where consistency isn't guaranteed.

The right design usually involves both: a vector database for semantic retrieval of unstructured content, and a structured database for precise retrieval of structured information. Keeping these separate and using each for what it's good at is simpler and more reliable than trying to do everything in one system.

Graph databases are worth knowing about for a specific case: when your domain has rich relationship structure that matters for reasoning. A knowledge graph that represents entities and their relationships can enable retrieval patterns that neither vector databases nor relational databases handle well.

Whether this applies to your use case depends heavily on the domain.

Memory Consistency

A problem that doesn't get enough attention: what happens when different parts of your memory system contain contradictory information?

A user tells the agent in one session that they prefer formal language. In a later session, they explicitly ask for casual language. Both preferences are now in long-term memory. Which one governs the current session?

Without explicit conflict resolution logic, the model will try to reconcile contradictions in ways that are not predictable. Building in recency weighting (more recent information takes precedence), explicit override flags, and periodic memory consolidation (where contradictions are resolved and the memory is updated) produces more reliable behavior.

Deciding What to Remember

One of the hardest practical questions in memory system design is: what gets stored?

Storing everything is expensive and leads to noisy retrieval. Storing only explicitly important information means you miss things that would have been valuable in hindsight.

A few principles that have worked well:

Store outcomes rather than just raw interactions. What worked? What didn't? What did the user actually use versus what they ignored?

Store summaries, not verbatim records, for long sessions. A well-designed summary captures the relevant information at a fraction of the storage cost and often retrieves better because it's been distilled.

Use recency weighting. Recent interactions are usually more relevant than distant ones.

Build in explicit forgetting. Information has a useful lifespan. Having TTL (time-to-live) policies for different types of stored information is good hygiene.

The Privacy Problem

Memory systems that store user information come with privacy obligations that deserve explicit attention.

What data are you collecting? What are you storing? Who has access to it? How long do you keep it? What do you do if a user asks you to delete their data?

GDPR, CCPA, and equivalent regulations in other jurisdictions may apply depending on where you operate and who your users are. Getting legal advice about your obligations in your specific context is strongly advisable before building a memory system that processes user data at scale.

More practically: users who are aware that their data is being stored and know how it's being used are more likely to trust the system. Being transparent about what you store and why, and giving users control over their data, is both ethically right and practically smart.

Chapter 10 Additional Content: Advanced Tool Design

Tool Design Patterns

Beyond the basics of tool definition, several design patterns come up repeatedly in production tool integrations.

The Facade Pattern wraps a complex API with a simpler interface that's easier for a language model to use correctly. If an API has many optional parameters, unusual error codes, or complex authentication requirements, wrapping it in a facade that handles these details and exposes a simpler interface improves model reliability significantly. The facade also provides a natural place to add logging, rate limiting, and error handling.

The Circuit Breaker Pattern prevents an agent from hammering a failing service with repeated calls. When a tool fails more than a threshold number of times in a short period, the circuit breaker opens and subsequent calls to that tool fail immediately with a clear "service unavailable" error, rather than making network calls that will also fail. This protects both the failing service and the agent's budget.

The Cache Pattern stores the results of tool calls and returns cached results for identical subsequent calls. This reduces latency and cost for frequently-repeated calls. Determining what to cache requires understanding which calls return deterministic results (cache indefinitely), which return results that change occasionally (cache with TTL), and which return results that change frequently or depend on current state (don't cache).

The Retry with Backoff Pattern handles transient failures by retrying failed calls with increasing delays between attempts. This is appropriate for failures that are likely temporary (network timeouts, rate limits) but not for failures that are likely permanent (authentication errors, malformed requests).

Distinguishing these failure types and applying the appropriate response is important.

Testing Tool Integrations

Tool integrations are where many production failures originate, and they deserve thorough testing.

Unit testing tool definitions: does the tool description accurately describe what the tool does, when to use it, and what format its outputs take? Test by providing the tool description to a model and asking it to describe the tool in its own words; if the description it produces doesn't match your intent, the definition needs work.

Integration testing with real tools: test tool calls with the actual underlying service, not just mocks. This catches issues like authentication failures, unexpected response formats, and rate limiting that mocks won't reveal.

Adversarial testing: try to get the model to call tools incorrectly. Give it ambiguous inputs, inputs that span multiple tool types, inputs that suggest using a tool for a purpose it's not designed for. The failures you discover this way are the ones that will occur in production.

Latency testing: measure tool call latency in realistic conditions, not just in a clean test environment. Network conditions, service load, and data size can all affect latency in ways that matter for user experience.

Tool Versioning and Migration

Tools change over time: APIs get updated, return formats change, new capabilities are added. Managing these changes in production requires careful version management.

When a tool's interface changes in a breaking way (different parameters, different return format), update the tool description to match. But also consider whether existing interactions stored in memory that reference the old tool behavior will be retrieved and confuse the model. Building tool version tags into memory records and filtering retrieved memories by tool version prevents this class of confusion.

Gradual migration from an old tool version to a new one is often safer than a hard cutover. Running both versions simultaneously and routing some fraction of calls to the new version while monitoring for differences in behavior lets you validate the new version before fully committing to it.

Building Tool Ecosystems

As an agentic system grows, the number of tools it has access to grows as well. At some scale, managing tool definitions becomes a significant engineering challenge.

A tool registry, a centralized store of tool definitions with version history, ownership metadata, and usage tracking, becomes valuable once you have more than a handful of tools. The registry makes it possible to understand what tools are available, who maintains them, how they're being used, and whether they're working correctly.

Tool discoverability is the problem of making it easy for agents to find and use relevant tools without being explicitly configured with every tool. Rather than listing all tools in every agent's context (which becomes expensive and noisy at scale), you can implement dynamic tool selection: given the current task, retrieve the most relevant tools from the registry and include only those in the agent's context. This is itself a retrieval problem and can be approached with the same techniques used for document retrieval.

Chapter 11 Additional Content: Memory Architecture in Practice

Implementing a Production Memory System

Moving from the conceptual framework to a working production memory system requires decisions about specific storage technologies, retrieval strategies, and operational practices.

For most production agentic systems, the memory stack looks like this: a relational database (PostgreSQL works well) for structured data like user profiles, task states, and explicit preferences; a vector database (Pinecone or Chroma) for semantic retrieval of unstructured content like documents and conversation summaries; and Redis or a similar key-value store for session-level state that needs to be fast to access.

The retrieval layer, which queries these stores and assembles the context for each model call, is where most of the interesting implementation work happens. A naive retrieval layer retrieves the top-K most semantically similar items from each store and concatenates them into the context. A more sophisticated retrieval layer considers relevance, recency, source type, and context length budget jointly.

Retrieval Budget Management

Language model context windows have a cost: more tokens means more expense and, for very long contexts, potential quality degradation. Managing how much context is used for memory retrieval is a real engineering challenge.

The retrieval budget needs to balance: the amount of context needed for the model to understand the current situation (necessary), the amount that helps the model perform better (valuable), and the amount that's irrelevant noise (harmful).

Finding this balance requires empirical testing, not just reasoning about it.

A practical approach: start with a conservative retrieval budget (say, 20% of the context window for retrieved memory), measure whether adding more retrieval improves quality, and calibrate to the maximum that produces quality improvement. Beyond that point, additional context doesn't help and starts to hurt.

Retrieval latency is also a budget: if retrieval adds 500ms to every model call, that might be acceptable or it might be a user experience problem depending on the context. Measuring retrieval latency separately from model call latency helps identify bottlenecks.

Memory Update Strategies

Deciding when and how to update memory is as important as deciding what to retrieve.

Synchronous updates happen during the model call: the model generates a response, and before the response is returned to the user, the memory system is updated with the relevant information from this interaction. This is simple and ensures memory is always current, but adds latency to every call.

Asynchronous updates happen in the background: the response is returned to the user immediately, and memory is updated asynchronously. This reduces latency for the user but means memory may be slightly stale. For most use cases, the latency benefit outweighs the staleness cost.

Batch updates accumulate changes and apply them periodically rather than after each interaction. This is efficient but means memory can be significantly stale. It's appropriate for infrequently-changing information (user preferences, domain knowledge) but not for rapidly-changing information (current task state).

Memory Compression

Over time, a system that stores everything it encounters will accumulate an enormous amount of memory. Retrieval quality degrades as the index grows, costs increase, and latency increases. Memory compression addresses this by reducing the amount stored while preserving the most valuable information.

Summarization-based compression periodically generates summaries of stored information and replaces the original content with the summary. A week's worth of daily conversation summaries might be compressed into a single summary of the week. This is lossy but preserves the most important information at a fraction of the storage cost.

Importance-weighted retention keeps information that was frequently retrieved or explicitly flagged as important and discards information that was rarely retrieved and never flagged. This requires tracking retrieval history, which adds a small amount of overhead but enables much more targeted retention.

Temporal discounting applies a recency factor to retrieval relevance: more recent information is considered more relevant than older information for the same query. This doesn't reduce storage but does reduce the impact of old information on retrieval, which has a similar practical effect.

Debugging Memory Systems

Memory systems produce some of the most confusing bugs in agentic systems because their effects are indirect: bad memory leads to bad model reasoning, which produces bad outputs, and tracing the chain from output back to memory requires careful logging.

The key logging practice: for every model call, log what was retrieved from memory and why (what query was used, what the relevance scores were). This makes it possible to answer the question "why did the model believe X?" by tracing back to what was in its context.

Memory audit tools that let you query the memory system directly, independently of the agent, are valuable for debugging. Being able to ask "what does the system know about user X?" and see the actual stored content helps identify cases where the memory is polluted, stale, or conflicting.

Common memory debugging scenarios: the model is behaving as if something is true that you never told it (check what's in memory for that topic), the model is behaving as if something is true that used to be true but isn't anymore (check for stale entries), the model is giving inconsistent answers (check for conflicting entries), the model's behavior has changed after a period of good performance (check whether the memory index has drifted due to accumulated entries).

Multi-Tenant Memory Isolation

When an agentic system serves multiple users or organizations, memory isolation becomes a security concern. User A's stored preferences, history, and data should not be retrievable when processing User B's requests.

Implementing this correctly requires tenant isolation at every layer of the memory stack: in the vector database (using separate namespaces or collections per tenant), in the relational database (using tenant ID as a filter on every query), and in the retrieval layer (enforcing that tenant context is always applied).

Testing tenant isolation is important and often skipped. Deliberately try to retrieve User A's data while processing a request in User B's context. If any data crosses tenant boundaries, you have a security vulnerability.

Chapter 10 Extended: Tool Ecosystems in Production

Building a Tool Library

As an agentic system matures, the collection of tools it uses grows from a handful to dozens or hundreds. Managing this at scale requires the same kind of engineering discipline you'd apply to a software library.

Documentation standards for tools deserve the same attention as documentation standards for code. A well-documented tool has: a precise description of what it does (not what it's for, but what it actually does), explicit preconditions (what must be true for the tool to work correctly), explicit postconditions (what will be true after the tool executes successfully), error conditions (what errors it can produce and what they mean), performance characteristics (typical latency, rate limits), and examples of correct and incorrect usage.

Tool coverage is the fraction of tasks in your system's domain that can be handled by available tools. Low coverage means the agent will frequently encounter tasks it cannot accomplish, either failing or hallucinating tool calls. Tracking coverage systematically, by analyzing failure logs for cases where the agent tried and failed to use a non-existent tool, tells you where to invest in new tool development.

Tool redundancy, having multiple tools that can accomplish similar goals, is valuable for resilience. If the primary search tool is down, a backup search tool can handle requests. If a specific API is rate-limited, an alternative data source can provide similar information. Designing tool sets with deliberate redundancy makes systems significantly more reliable.

Tool Composition Patterns

Individual tools accomplish specific narrow tasks. Real agent workflows often require combining tools in sequences, where the output of one tool becomes the input of another.

The data enrichment pattern: start with a basic record, retrieve additional information from multiple sources, combine the results into an enriched record. A customer support agent might start with a customer ID, retrieve the account history from the CRM, retrieve recent interactions from the support system, retrieve the customer's product configuration from the product database, and combine all of this into a rich context for the support interaction.

The validate-then-act pattern: retrieve or generate data, validate it meets requirements, then take action based on validated data. A content publishing agent might generate a draft, validate it against style guidelines and policy rules, and only publish if it passes validation. The validation step prevents the action step from running with bad data.

The fallback chain pattern: try the primary approach, and if it fails, try progressively simpler or more expensive alternatives. A research agent might first try to answer a question from its memory, then from an internal knowledge base, then from a web search, and only ask for human input if all automated approaches fail.

These patterns can be encoded in the orchestration logic (code) or described to the agent in its system prompt. Code is more reliable; system prompt descriptions rely on the model following them correctly. For high-stakes tool composition sequences, encoding in code is worth the additional implementation effort.

Rate Limiting and Quota Management

Production tool integrations need to manage rate limits and quotas. Most external APIs have rate limits; exceeding them causes failures. Most paid APIs have quotas that affect cost.

Implementing rate limiting at the tool layer rather than relying on agents to manage their own rate limits is more reliable. A rate limiter that enforces per-tool, per-time-window call limits prevents agents from hammering APIs regardless of how they decide to use tools.

Quota monitoring, tracking how much of monthly or daily quotas has been used and alerting when approaching limits, prevents unexpected outages due to quota exhaustion. For high-value APIs, setting soft limits that alert at 80% of quota and hard limits that prevent calls above 95% gives time to respond before the quota is fully exhausted.

Cost tracking by tool is also valuable: which tools are most expensive? Are they being called efficiently? Are there opportunities to reduce costs by caching results or batching calls? This analysis requires attribution of costs to specific tool calls, which is straightforward if tool calls are logged with cost information.

Chapter 10 Further Extended: Real-World Tool Integration Examples

Web Search Integration

Web search is one of the most commonly used tools in agentic systems and one of the most commonly misimplemented. A few patterns worth knowing.

The query reformulation pattern: rather than using the user's input directly as a search query, have the agent generate a search-optimized version of the query. Natural language questions ("what is the best way to handle authentication in a

LangGraph application?") often don't produce good search results; reformulating them as search queries ("LangGraph authentication best practices 2024") does.

The result quality filtering pattern: web search returns results with varying quality. Implementing a filter that checks result quality (is this from a reputable source? Is it recent enough? Does it seem relevant?) before including results in the agent's context improves the quality of retrieved information significantly.

The multi-query pattern: complex questions often benefit from multiple search queries covering different aspects of the question, rather than a single query trying to cover everything. An agent researching a market might run separate queries for market size data, key players, recent trends, and regulatory context, then synthesize the results.

Database Query Integration

Integrating database queries as agent tools requires careful design to be both safe and useful.

Schema documentation in the tool definition is essential: the agent needs to know what tables exist, what columns they contain, and what the relationships between tables are. Without this, the agent will generate queries that reference tables or columns that don't exist.

Query validation before execution, checking that the generated query is syntactically valid and only references existing tables and columns, prevents most query generation errors from causing database errors.

Read-only enforcement, running agent-generated queries with database credentials that only allow SELECT statements, prevents accidental data modification. Even if the agent generates a destructive query (which well-designed agents shouldn't, but production systems encounter many edge cases), read-only credentials prevent it from executing.

Result size limiting prevents agents from accidentally retrieving entire large tables. Setting a maximum result size and returning an error with a clear message when the query exceeds it prompts the agent to add more specific filters.

Chapter 11 Extended: Advanced Memory Patterns

Session Memory Architecture

Session memory, the working state of a conversation or task that persists across multiple model calls within a session but not across sessions, is the most operationally critical layer of the memory stack because it's what makes conversations feel coherent.

The naive approach to session memory is to accumulate the full conversation history and pass it all in every call. This works for short sessions but breaks down for long ones: the context gets expensive, and important information from early in the session can get lost in the middle of a very long context.

A more sophisticated approach is selective context management: rather than including everything, include a summarized version of the early conversation plus the full recent conversation. The summary captures the most important context from earlier without consuming the entire context window. As the conversation progresses, the boundary between "summarized" and "full detail" moves forward.

The implementation: after each N turns (where N is a tunable parameter), summarize the oldest M turns into a compressed summary. Store the summary and discard the full turn records. The context for subsequent calls is: the system prompt, the session summary, and the most recent K turns in full detail.

Cross-Session Context

Building persistent context that carries across sessions requires careful design about what to carry and how to represent it.

User profiles in long-term memory accumulate information about user preferences, common task types, and relevant background. Rather than retrieving this in full on every call, retrieve selectively based on what's relevant to the current task.

Task continuation context is needed when a user returns to continue a multi-session task. The agent needs to know what was accomplished in previous sessions, what's still to be done, and any relevant context from past work. Storing explicit session summaries with task-progress annotations makes this retrieval more reliable.

Project-level context accumulates knowledge about an ongoing project across many sessions. A software project might accumulate understanding of the architecture, coding conventions, key decisions made and why, and known issues. Structuring this knowledge explicitly (rather than hoping to retrieve it from session summaries) makes it much more reliably usable.

Associative Memory

Beyond semantic similarity retrieval, associative memory retrieves based on relationships between concepts. When the agent encounters a customer complaint about a specific product issue, associative memory might retrieve: the relevant product documentation, previous complaints about similar issues, the resolutions that worked for those complaints, and any known bugs or limitations associated with the product.

Implementing associative memory requires explicit relationship modeling, either through a graph database that stores entity relationships or through metadata annotations on stored items that specify their relationships to other stored items.

For many use cases, a simpler approximation works well: store items with rich metadata tags and implement multi-field retrieval that combines semantic similarity with metadata matching. This is more practical than a full graph database for most production systems.

Memory and Context Management for Long-Running Tasks

For tasks that run over hours or days rather than minutes, memory architecture requires special attention. The task might run across many sessions, involve many individual operations, and accumulate significant context that needs to be available for future operations.

A checkpoint pattern for long-running tasks: at defined intervals (end of each work session, or after each major phase of the task), generate a checkpoint that captures: what has been accomplished, what's still to be done, any important findings or decisions made, any problems encountered and how they were handled, and the current state of all in-progress work.

These checkpoints serve as resumption points. When the task resumes after an interruption, loading the most recent checkpoint gives the agent enough context to pick up where it left off without requiring all the context from every preceding step.

Checkpoint granularity affects both storage cost and resumption quality. Fine-grained checkpoints (after every tool call) give more precise resumption but at high storage cost. Coarse-grained checkpoints (after each major phase) are cheaper but may require more work to resume after an interruption. The right granularity depends on the task duration and the cost of redoing work after a failure.

SECTION III: Scaling, Strategy, and Orchestration

Chapter 12

Multi-Agent Systems

The premise behind multi-agent systems is that some problems are better solved by several specialized agents working together than by one general agent trying to do everything. This is true for some problems, and people sometimes apply it to problems where it's not.

When Multiple Agents Make Sense

The clearest case for multiple agents is when the task genuinely requires different types of expertise or different access profiles.

A research and report-writing pipeline has natural seams: gathering sources is different from analyzing them, which is different from synthesizing them into prose, which is different from checking the result for accuracy. Each step benefits from optimization for that specific task, and they're sufficiently independent that they can be developed and tested separately.

A customer service system that handles different types of requests, billing, technical support, sales, escalation, naturally decomposes into specialized agents that handle each domain, with a routing layer that sends requests to the right place. Each specialized agent can be tuned to the specific knowledge and tone required for its domain.

A system with different access privileges, some users can see sensitive data, others can't, benefits from having separate agents with appropriate access rather than one agent that has to implement access control through prompt logic.

The case against is simpler: coordination overhead is real. Every time agents have to communicate, you're adding calls, adding latency, and adding potential for miscommunication.

For a task that one well-designed agent can handle, the multi-agent approach is just slower and more complex.

There's also a debugging complexity argument against multi-agent systems that often goes underweighted. When something goes wrong in a single-agent system, you have one system to examine. When something goes wrong in a multi-agent system, the failure could be in any of the agents or in the coordination between them. The additional diagnostic surface area is a real cost.

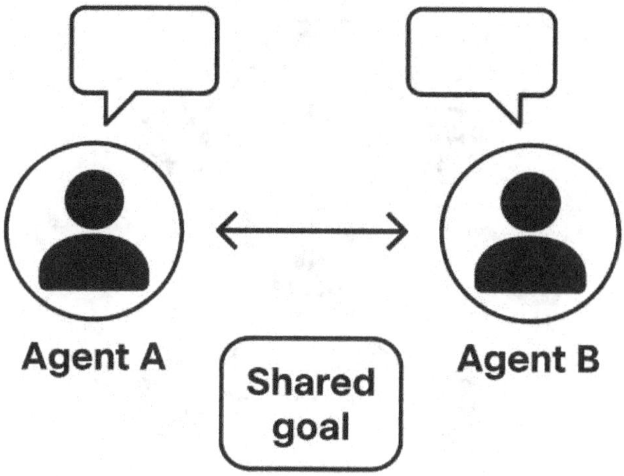

Designing Agent Interfaces

When building multi-agent systems, the interfaces between agents deserve as much attention as the agents themselves. How does information flow from one agent to another? What format does it take? How are errors communicated?

I've found that defining explicit interface contracts between agents, specifying the expected inputs and outputs for each agent, is one of the highest-leverage things you can do for multi-agent system reliability. When interfaces are implicit, agents end up making assumptions about what they'll receive and what format to produce that don't always hold, and failures at the interface boundaries are some of the hardest to diagnose.

Testing interfaces independently, before testing the full multi-agent interaction, is worth the effort. Can you give agent B the kind of output that agent A is supposed to produce and verify that agent B handles it correctly? This narrows down where failures occur and makes the development cycle faster.

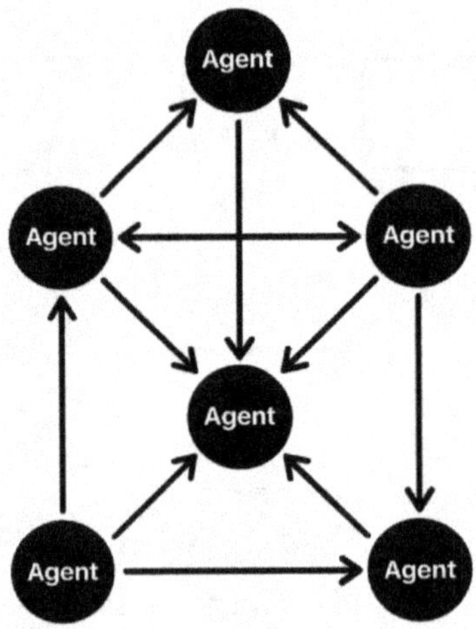

Multi-agent system layout

Communication Patterns

How agents communicate with each other determines a lot about system reliability.

The simplest pattern is sequential: agent A produces output, passes it to agent B, B produces output, passes it to C. This is easy to reason about and easy to debug. The cost is that it's slow, each step waits for the previous one to complete, and failures propagate linearly through the chain.

Parallel patterns let multiple agents work simultaneously on independent parts of a task, with a synthesis step that combines the results. Faster, but requires careful design to make sure the parallel components are actually independent and that the synthesis step handles cases where some components fail or produce low-quality outputs.

The hub-and-spoke pattern has a coordinator agent that manages all communication between worker agents rather than having workers communicate directly. This centralizes coordination logic, which makes it easier to maintain visibility into system state and to handle failures, but it makes the coordinator a bottleneck and a single point of failure.

In practice, the pattern I use most is a light version of hub-and-spoke: a coordinator that holds the plan and manages handoffs between workers, but workers that can communicate results back to the coordinator rather than going through an intermediary for every message. Enough centralization to maintain coherent state, not so much that the coordinator becomes a bottleneck.

Handling Partial Failures

Multi-agent systems need explicit logic for partial failures: what happens when one agent in a pipeline fails or produces poor output?

In a sequential pipeline, a failure in agent B stops everything downstream. Depending on your use case, you might want to: retry the failed step, skip it and continue with reduced output, substitute a fallback result, or abort the whole task. Each strategy is appropriate in different contexts, and specifying it explicitly rather than letting errors propagate unhandled is important.

In parallel pipelines, the synthesis step needs to handle cases where some agents failed. Can it produce a partial result? Should it flag that some components are missing? Should it abort if any component failed? These questions should be answered in the design, not discovered in production.

Building in checkpoints, places where the coordinator evaluates whether it's safe to proceed based on the quality of outputs received so far, is a pattern that improves reliability significantly. It costs some efficiency (you're adding evaluation calls) but saves the cost of completing a long pipeline only to discover at the end that an early step produced an error that invalidated everything downstream.

Shared Context and State

The hardest problem in multi-agent systems is maintaining consistent shared state. Each agent has its own context window, which means each agent's view of the world can diverge from the others'.

Building explicit state management that's shared across agents, rather than relying on each agent's context, significantly reduces this class of problems. A shared task log that all agents can read and write to, with explicit write ordering to prevent conflicts, is the most common approach.

The shared state should include not just what has been done but what has been tried and failed. An agent that doesn't know that another agent already tried a particular approach and found it insufficient will waste time repeating the attempt. Logging failed approaches to the shared state, not just successful ones, prevents this.

Debugging Multi-Agent Systems

Multi-agent systems are significantly harder to debug than single-agent ones. When something goes wrong, the failure may have originated several steps back, with effects that propagated through multiple agents before becoming visible.

The most important practice is comprehensive logging: every agent call, every message passed between agents, every tool call, every state update. The overhead is real but the alternative, debugging with limited visibility, is much worse.

Building in "explain mode" is useful: a way to replay a session with additional logging that shows what each agent was thinking at each step. This is expensive to run routinely but invaluable when debugging specific failures.

Isolating agent behaviors for testing helps: can you test each agent independently with controlled inputs, before testing the multi-agent interaction? If you can, you can narrow down whether a failure is in an individual agent or in the interaction between agents, which makes diagnosis much faster.

Chapter 13

Evaluation and Feedback

Evaluation is where a lot of agentic systems fail to mature. Building the initial system is exciting; instrumenting it well enough to know if it's actually working as intended is tedious and often underinvested.

What to Evaluate

The obvious thing to evaluate is output quality: are the outputs the system produces good? But for agentic systems, "good" is often multidimensional in ways that matter for how you instrument your evaluation.

Task completion rate: does the agent successfully finish the tasks it's given? This is the most basic metric, but it needs to be defined carefully. "Successfully finished" can mean anything from "returned some output" to "completed the task correctly in a way the user found useful." These are very different, and conflating them produces misleading metrics.

Output quality: when the task is completed, how good is the result? For tasks with objective criteria, you can measure against ground truth. For tasks with subjective criteria, you typically need human evaluation or an LLM-as-judge approach.

Efficiency: how many calls, how much time, how much cost did it take? A system that produces good outputs but takes ten times longer and costs ten times more than it should isn't ready for production.

Failure modes: how does the system fail, and how often? Knowing that a system fails 5% of the time is less useful than knowing it fails 20% of the time on a specific class of inputs and 1% on others. The distribution of failures tells you where to focus improvement effort.

There are also operational metrics worth tracking: escalation rate (how often does the system involve a human?), retry rate (how often does the system retry a failed step?), latency distribution (not just average but percentiles, since tail latencies matter for user experience), and cost per task.

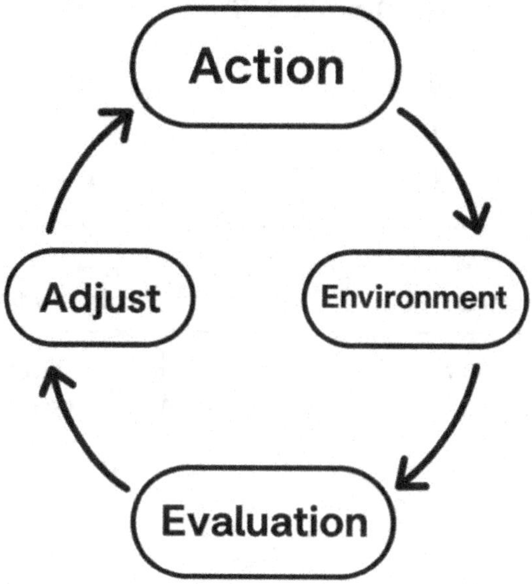

Evaluation at Multiple Levels

For complex agentic systems, evaluation needs to happen at multiple levels, not just at the final output.

Component-level evaluation checks whether individual agents or tools are working correctly in isolation. Does the retrieval component return relevant results? Does the summarizer produce coherent summaries? Does the validator catch the types of errors it's supposed to catch? Component-level failures often explain system-level failures, and catching them at the component level is much faster.

Integration-level evaluation checks whether the components work correctly together. Does the coordinator produce plans that the workers can execute? Does the output from one agent flow correctly into the next? Are there systematic mismatches at the interfaces?

System-level evaluation checks whether the end-to-end behavior is correct. This is what users experience, but it's also the hardest place to diagnose problems because a system-level failure can have many possible causes.

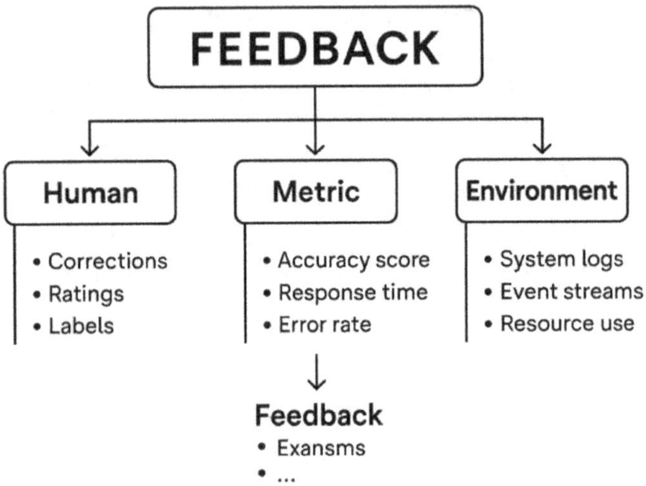

LLM-as-Judge

For tasks where human evaluation is too expensive to do at scale, using an LLM to evaluate the outputs of your agent is a practical approach. The LLM reviewer is given a rubric and asked to evaluate whether the output meets specific criteria.

This works reasonably well for many cases, but there are important limitations. LLM judges have their own biases: they tend to prefer longer, more verbose responses, they tend to be overconfident in factual claims, and their evaluations are not always consistent across runs.

Using LLM judges as a rough filter rather than a precise metric is more defensible than treating their scores as ground truth.

For high-stakes evaluation, combine LLM-based and human evaluation: use the LLM to handle the bulk of the evaluation and flag borderline cases for human review.

One refinement that improves LLM judge reliability: ask the judge to explain its reasoning before giving a score. The explanation step forces the model to think through the evaluation more carefully and tends to produce more consistent and accurate scores.

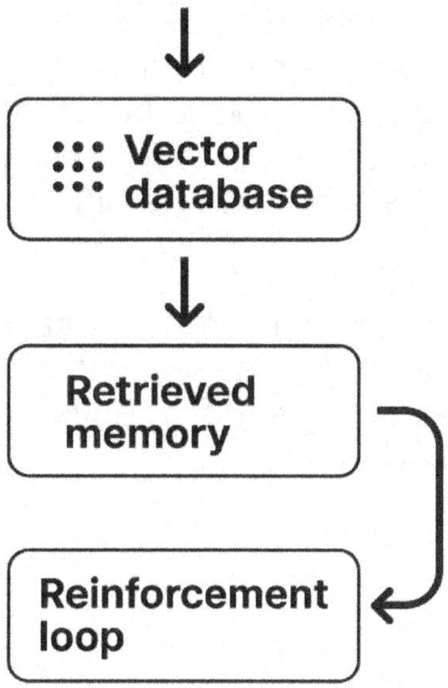

Building a Feedback Loop

The point of evaluation is to improve the system, and improvement requires a feedback loop: evaluation, insight, intervention, re-evaluation.

The most common and often most effective interventions are changes to the system prompt and retrieval strategy, because they're fast to implement and test. Model changes are more expensive and take longer to validate. Fine-tuning has the highest potential upside but requires data collection, training, and rigorous evaluation to be worth the effort.

Building the feedback loop explicitly means establishing cadence: how often do you review evaluation results? What thresholds trigger intervention? Who is responsible for acting on the evaluation? Systems without this structure tend to get evaluated once after launch and then left to drift.

The Evaluation Cold Start Problem

When you're first building a system, you often don't have labeled data or established baselines. The approach that works best: start with a small, hand-evaluated test set, maybe 50-100 examples, where you've personally evaluated what a good response looks like. Build your evaluation infrastructure around this small set. As you gather more production data, expand the test set.

The early test set won't be representative. That's fine. The goal is to establish a baseline you can move relative to and to catch obvious regressions, not to have a statistically rigorous evaluation from day one.

Chapter 14

Human-in-the-Loop and Delegation Design

The question of when to involve a human, and how, is one of the more important design decisions in any agentic system. Get it wrong in either direction and you either have a system that's constantly interrupting users for unnecessary confirmations or one that makes consequential decisions it shouldn't be trusted with.

When to Involve a Human

High-stakes, irreversible actions. Sending a formal communication to an important external party. Making a financial transaction. Deleting data. Publishing something publicly. The common thread is that the cost of a mistake is high and the action can't be undone. For these, explicit human approval, not just logging, is the right default.

Low-confidence situations. When the agent's confidence in the right action is below a threshold you've established, involving a human is cheaper than making a mistake. Calibrating confidence thresholds requires empirical observation of where the model is actually right and wrong, rather than where it says it is confident.

Novel situations. The first time a system encounters a situation significantly different from what it was designed for, human review is warranted even if the agent's confidence is high. Building a mechanism to flag novelty, "this input looks different from previous inputs in ways I can't fully characterize," is useful.

Cases where the stakes of being wrong are asymmetric. If the cost of a false negative (failing to take an action that should have been taken) is much higher than the cost of a false positive (taking an action unnecessarily), err toward human confirmation.

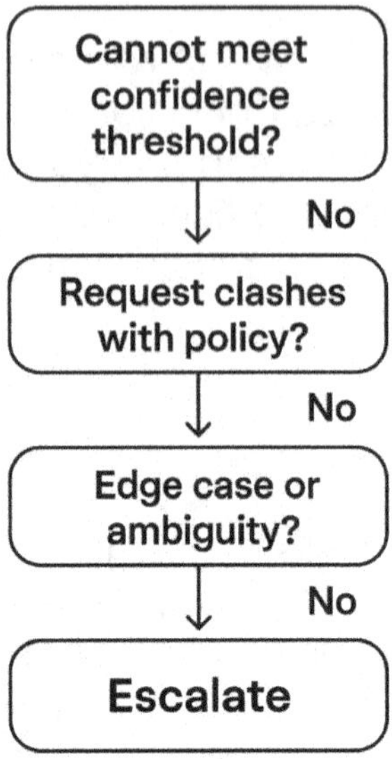

Designing Escalation Triggers

Escalation triggers, the conditions under which the system involves a human, should be designed explicitly rather than left to the model's judgment. Relying on the model to decide when to escalate is unreliable because models are overconfident and may not recognize when they're in a situation they shouldn't handle autonomously.

Explicit triggers include: confidence below a threshold, action reversibility class above a threshold, presence of specific keywords or entity types in the input, task type not seen in training data, or any combination of these.

Building the escalation trigger logic in code rather than in the system prompt is more reliable. Code-level checks that run before irreversible actions are taken, regardless of what the model has decided, provide a safety net that prompt-level instructions cannot.

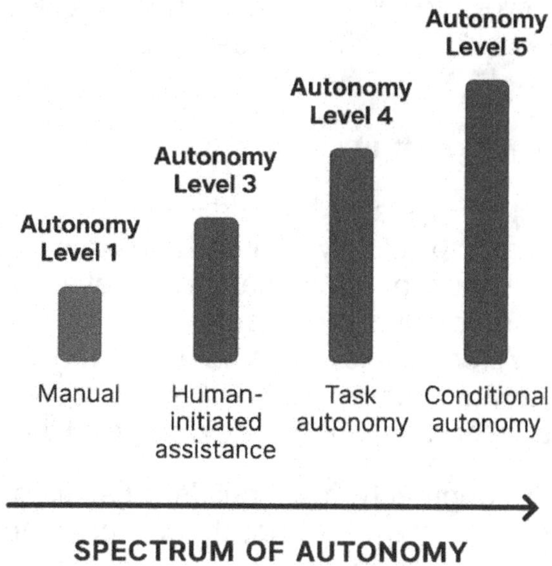

Designing the Handoff

When the system does involve a human, how it does so matters significantly for the user experience and for whether the human can actually be useful.

The worst handoffs are vague: "I'm not sure what to do here. Please advise." The human doesn't know what the agent tried, what it knows, or what options are available.

Better handoffs are specific: "I need to decide whether to send this email to the client now or wait until I have the Q4 numbers, which should be available tomorrow. The email is urgent per the client's request, but including the Q4 data would make it more useful. My recommendation is to wait, but I wanted to confirm. Here is the draft email, and here is what I know about the Q4 timeline."

The principle is that a good handoff should be legible: the human should be able to understand the situation, evaluate the options, and make a decision without having to dig into system logs or reconstruct context. If your handoffs require human reviewers to investigate further before they can be useful, your handoffs are poorly designed.

Graduated Autonomy

Most production systems should start with more human involvement and gradually reduce it as confidence in the system builds. Launch with human review of all outputs. Track which types of outputs are consistently approved without modification. After a sufficient sample size, move those output types to automated delivery without review. Continue tracking, and if quality degrades, bring review back for those types.

This gradual approach also builds trust with users and stakeholders. A system that has been operating reliably for three months, with documented accuracy and a clear audit trail, is much easier to extend to new capabilities than one that immediately tried to do everything autonomously.

The Feedback Value of Human Oversight

There's a secondary benefit to human oversight that's worth making explicit: it generates labeled data. Every time a human reviews an agent output and accepts, rejects, or modifies it, they're creating a labeled example that can inform future improvements.

Capturing this feedback systematically, storing what was reviewed, what the human decision was, and if they modified it, what the modification was, creates a dataset that can be used for evaluation, for fine-tuning, and for identifying systematic problems. This makes the oversight not just a safety mechanism but an investment in future system quality.

Chapter 15

Governance, Safety, and Alignment

This chapter covers territory that tends to be either underemphasized (in teams that are moving fast and treating safety as a future problem) or over-philosophized (in discussions that focus on speculative long-term risks rather than practical near-term ones). I'll try to focus on what actually matters for production systems today.

What Can Go Wrong

Four main failure categories come up in practice, and knowing them helps focus improvement effort.

Capability failures: the system doesn't do what it's supposed to. Wrong answers, missed cases, poor output quality. These are the most common failure mode and usually the easiest to fix.

Reliability failures: the system works in testing and fails in production, or works for some inputs and fails for others in ways that aren't obvious from testing. Usually a combination of insufficient test coverage and distribution shift.

Safety failures: the system takes actions that cause harm, to users, to third parties, or to the organization running it. This includes obvious things like generating harmful content, less obvious things like providing incorrect information in high-stakes contexts, and subtle things like reinforcing harmful behaviors over time.

Alignment failures: the system does what it's optimized to do, but what it's optimized to do turns out not to be what you actually want. The system is working as designed; the design is wrong.

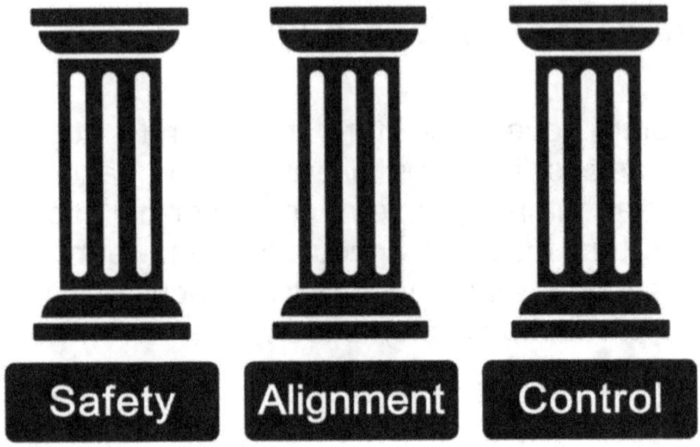

Practical Safety for Production Systems

Content filtering: systems that generate or process user-facing content should have filtering for obviously harmful outputs. This is imperfect but important.

Access control: agents should have the minimum permissions necessary to do their job. An agent that needs to read customer records for support purposes doesn't need to modify them. Implementing least-privilege access requires careful thought about what each agent actually needs and deliberate restriction of everything else.

Audit trails: every consequential action taken by an agent should be logged with enough context to reconstruct what happened and why. This is important for debugging, for compliance, and for accountability.

Rate limiting and cost controls: agents that can make many API calls need throttling to prevent runaway costs from bugs or adversarial inputs.

Human escalation paths: every agent should have a well-defined process for escalating to a human when it encounters something it can't handle safely. This path should be tested; a theoretical escalation mechanism that doesn't actually work in practice is not useful.

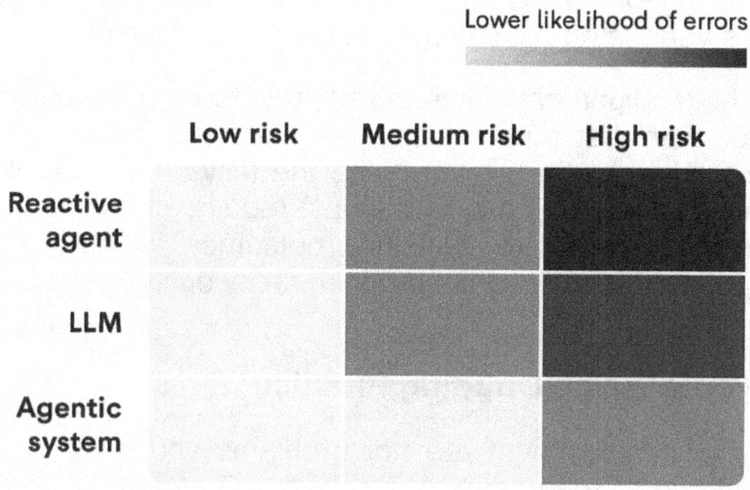

Safety as Architecture

The framing of safety as an afterthought, something you add after the system works, consistently produces worse outcomes than treating it as an architectural concern from the start.

When safety requirements are defined upfront, they shape decisions about what tools the agent can access, what actions it can take autonomously, how it handles uncertainty, and how it communicates its limitations. These are design decisions, not features. Retrofitting them after the fact requires changing fundamental aspects of the system rather than adding a layer on top.

Alignment in Practice

The practical alignment question for most agentic systems is: is the system actually optimizing for what you want, or is it optimizing for a proxy that correlates with what you want in the cases you tested but diverges in cases you didn't?

Catching alignment failures requires looking at outcomes rather than just outputs: are users actually better off after interacting with the system? Are the tasks that "completed" actually useful? These questions require connecting your evaluation metrics to real-world outcomes, which is harder than measuring things the model directly optimizes for.

Governance as Ongoing Practice

Safety and alignment are not problems you solve once at launch and then move on from. Systems operate in environments that change. User behaviors change. Attack patterns evolve. The model's behavior may shift as the provider updates the underlying model.

The teams that handle this well treat governance as an ongoing practice: regular review of evaluation metrics and failure patterns, periodic audits of system behavior, a process for incorporating new information about failure modes, and clear ownership for decisions about when to restrict or expand system capabilities.

The teams that handle it poorly treat governance as a launch checklist. This tends to work until it doesn't, and when it doesn't, the consequences tend to be proportional to how long the problem was allowed to accumulate.

Chapter 12 Additional Content: Multi-Agent Coordination Patterns

Negotiation Between Agents

Some multi-agent tasks require agents to negotiate with each other: to agree on a shared approach, to resolve conflicting assessments, or to coordinate resource allocation. This is more complex than simple delegation and requires specific design patterns.

The simplest negotiation pattern is voting: each agent independently produces an assessment, and the coordinator takes the majority or highest-confidence view. This works well when the agents have genuinely independent perspectives and the task is assessment rather than action.

A more structured negotiation pattern is the proposal-critique cycle: one agent produces a proposal, another critiques it, the first agent revises based on the critique, and this continues until both agents are satisfied or a maximum number of rounds is reached. This is more expensive than voting but produces more thoroughly vetted outputs for complex tasks.

For resource allocation (deciding which agent handles which task when tasks compete for resources), priority-based allocation is the simplest approach: define task priorities explicitly and route tasks to agents based on priority. When agents have different capabilities, capability-weighted allocation routes tasks to the most capable available agent rather than the highest-priority task.

Message Passing Protocols

In multi-agent systems where agents communicate directly with each other rather than through a central coordinator, message passing protocols define how messages are structured and how agents respond to them.

The most common failure mode in message passing systems is message misinterpretation: agent A sends a message intended in one way, agent B interprets it differently. This leads to behaviors that are hard to debug because both agents may be behaving correctly given their interpretation, but the system as a whole is producing wrong outputs.

Structured message formats significantly reduce misinterpretation. Rather than passing free-form text between agents, define message schemas: what fields does a task assignment message have? What fields does a completion report have? What fields does an escalation message have? Having explicit schemas forces clarity about what's being communicated.

Message validation, checking that received messages conform to the expected schema before processing them, catches misformatted messages early and produces clear error messages rather than mysterious downstream failures.

Agent Specialization Depth

How specialized should individual agents be? Very specialized agents are good at narrow tasks but require more coordination overhead. Generalist agents require less coordination but perform less well on any specific task.

The right level of specialization depends on: task heterogeneity (how different are the tasks in your system?), task volume (are there enough tasks of each type to justify specialized agents?), and coordination cost (how much overhead does adding another agent add?).

A practical heuristic: start with fewer, more general agents and split them when you identify specific task types that would benefit from specialized prompts, specialized tools, or specialized access profiles. Splitting agents based on observed need is safer than trying to predict the right specialization upfront.

Chapter 13 Additional Content: Evaluation Infrastructure

Building an Evaluation Pipeline

A complete evaluation pipeline for an agentic system has several stages.

Data collection: gathering inputs, outputs, and metadata for evaluation. For production systems, this means logging all model calls with their context and outputs. For test systems, this means building a representative test set that covers the range of cases the system needs to handle.

Ground truth labeling: for metrics that require comparison against expected outputs, you need labeled examples. This is expensive for human labeling and imperfect for LLM-based labeling. Investing in a small, high-quality human-labeled set that you trust, and using that as the reference for comparing different system versions, is usually better than relying entirely on LLM-based evaluation.

Metric computation: running the evaluation metrics against collected data. This should be automated so it can be run continuously without manual effort.

Result analysis: turning raw metric values into actionable insights. This is where human judgment is most needed: a metric degraded by 3%, but is that a meaningful signal or noise? Which specific inputs drove the degradation?

Reporting and alerting: making evaluation results visible to the people who need to act on them, and triggering alerts when metrics drop below thresholds.

Evaluating Agentic Behavior Specifically

Standard LLM evaluation focuses on output quality for individual calls. Agentic evaluation additionally needs to assess multi-step behavior: does the agent plan well? Does it recover from failures? Does it know when to escalate?

Planning quality evaluation: given a goal, how good is the plan the agent generates? This requires either human evaluation of plan quality or an automated rubric (does the plan include the required steps? Are dependencies correctly identified?).

Recovery behavior evaluation: when a tool fails or returns unexpected results, does the agent recover gracefully? Inject deliberate failures and assess whether the agent recovers, escalates, or fails in unhelpful ways.

Escalation quality evaluation: when the agent escalates, is it escalating for the right reasons? Tracking what situations trigger escalations and whether those situations actually warranted escalation helps calibrate thresholds.

Efficiency evaluation: how many steps does the agent take to complete a task? More steps usually means more cost and latency. Comparing step counts across different system versions helps identify whether changes made the agent more or less efficient.

Evaluation Pitfalls

A few common evaluation mistakes worth avoiding.

Evaluating on your training distribution: if your test set consists of examples similar to what you optimized for, you'll get inflated performance numbers. Including genuinely novel examples in your evaluation catches generalization failures that in-distribution evaluation misses.

Optimizing for metrics at the expense of actual quality: once you define a metric, there's pressure to improve it, and sometimes the easiest way to improve the metric is to optimize for the metric specifically rather than improving actual quality. Periodic human evaluation of raw outputs, independent of any metric, helps detect this.

Evaluating only happy-path behavior: most evaluation is done on normal inputs. But most production failures happen on abnormal inputs. Deliberately including edge cases, adversarial inputs, and inputs near the boundaries of the system's design scope in your evaluation is important.

Chapter 14 Additional Content: Delegation Pattern Library

Common Delegation Patterns

Several delegation patterns come up repeatedly across different domains.

The Expert Routing Pattern delegates different types of requests to specialized agents based on the request type. A general-purpose coordinator receives all requests, classifies them, and routes to the appropriate specialist. The value is specialization: each specialist can be optimized for its specific task type without compromising its ability to handle other types.

The Quality Assurance Pattern pairs each primary agent with a QA agent that reviews its outputs before they're passed along. The QA agent checks against defined quality criteria and either approves the output or sends it back for revision. This adds cost but significantly improves output reliability for tasks where quality matters.

The Confidence Escalation Pattern routes requests to progressively more capable (and expensive) agents based on confidence scores. A cheap, fast agent handles the request first. If its confidence in the output is above a threshold, the output is returned. If not, the request is routed to a more capable agent. This optimizes cost by using expensive agents only when cheaper ones aren't sufficient.

The Human-as-Agent Pattern treats human reviewers as agents in the system, with defined interfaces (request format, expected response format, latency SLA). This makes human involvement explicit and manageable rather than an ad-hoc interruption to an otherwise automated system.

Configuring Delegation Thresholds

Delegation threshold configuration determines when the system routes to a more capable agent or escalates to a human. Getting these thresholds right requires empirical observation.

The process: deploy with conservative thresholds (escalate frequently), collect data on what's being escalated and whether the escalation was warranted, identify cases where escalation was unnecessary (the simpler agent would have handled it correctly), and relax the threshold for those cases. Repeat until the escalation rate is calibrated to the appropriate level.

Track false positives (unnecessary escalations) and false negatives (cases that should have been escalated but weren't) separately. These suggest different interventions: too many false positives means the threshold is too conservative, too many false negatives means the threshold is too permissive.

Chapter 15 Additional Content: Operational Safety Practices

Red-Teaming Agentic Systems

Red-teaming, deliberately trying to get a system to misbehave, is a valuable safety practice that's often skipped for agentic systems because it seems like more work than for simpler systems. It's actually more important for agentic systems because the consequences of misbehavior are larger.

Prompt injection attacks: try to get the system to follow instructions embedded in user inputs or retrieved content that override its designed behavior. Can you get the system to take actions it shouldn't by embedding instructions in a document it processes?

Boundary violation attempts: try to get the system to take actions outside its designed scope. Can you get a customer service agent to access accounts other than the one specified? Can you get a content generation agent to produce content it's supposed to refuse?

Escalation avoidance: try to get the system to handle situations it should escalate. Can you phrase a request in ways that prevent the system from recognizing it should involve a human?

Resource exhaustion: try to get the system to use more resources than intended. Can you craft a request that causes the agent to make many API calls, run for a long time, or generate very large outputs?

Document the results of red-teaming exercises and use them to improve the system's defenses. A system that passes a red-teaming exercise has not proven it's safe; it's proven it survived the specific attacks you tried. Ongoing red-teaming as the system evolves is important.

Incident Response for Agentic Systems

When an agentic system causes a problem in production, the incident response process needs to be adapted to the specific properties of agentic systems.

The first priority is containment: if the system is taking actions with real consequences, stopping those actions quickly is more important than understanding why they're happening.

Having a kill switch, a mechanism to immediately suspend all autonomous action, is important and should be tested before it's needed.

The second priority is understanding: what actions did the system take, in what order, based on what reasoning? This requires detailed logs of every agent call and every action taken. Without these logs, reconstructing what happened is very difficult.

The third priority is correction: if the system took incorrect actions, what needs to be undone? Reversible actions can be rolled back. Irreversible actions (sent emails, published content, financial transactions) cannot, but their effects might be mitigated with human intervention.

The fourth priority is prevention: why did the system take the incorrect actions, and what changes prevent it from happening again? This requires a root cause analysis that traces the failure back to its origin: was it a model error, a tool failure, a missing governance rule, a gap in the escalation logic?

Building Safety Culture

Technical safety measures are necessary but not sufficient. The teams operating agentic systems also need to maintain a culture that takes safety seriously.

This means: reporting near-misses (cases where the system almost did something wrong) even if no harm resulted, conducting regular reviews of system behavior looking for concerning patterns, maintaining skepticism about impressive performance numbers (are we actually safe, or have we just been lucky?), and prioritizing safety improvements over feature additions when they're in conflict.

It also means: being honest with stakeholders about what the system can and can't do safely, resisting pressure to expand autonomy faster than the evidence supports, and being willing to roll back capabilities when problems are discovered.

The teams that do this well are the ones that treat safety incidents as learning opportunities rather than failures to hide. Every incident that occurs despite their best efforts is information about where the system design needs improvement. Using that information systematically is what separates teams that build increasingly reliable systems from teams that keep encountering the same types of problems.

Chapter 12 Extended: Multi-Agent System Design Patterns

Blackboard Architecture

The blackboard architecture is a classic multi-agent pattern that works well for problems where multiple specialized agents contribute to a shared solution incrementally.

In a blackboard system, there's a shared data structure (the "blackboard") that all agents can read from and write to. Each agent monitors the blackboard for situations where it can contribute, performs its work, and writes its output back to the blackboard. A controller manages the overall process, deciding which agent to activate based on the current state of the blackboard.

This pattern is useful for knowledge synthesis tasks: building up a comprehensive understanding of a complex topic, where different specialized agents contribute expertise in different areas. A market research system might have agents specialized in different industries, data types (quantitative vs qualitative), and geographic regions, all contributing to a shared research output.

The implementation requires careful design of the blackboard schema: what information can be stored there, how is it organized, how do agents indicate that a piece of information is complete versus provisional? Sloppy blackboard design leads to agents stepping on each other's work or failing to integrate their contributions coherently.

Market-Based Coordination

In some multi-agent systems, tasks are allocated through a market-like bidding mechanism rather than through hierarchical delegation. Each task is offered to available agents, agents bid on tasks based on their perceived capability and availability, and the task is assigned to the winning bidder.

This approach is useful when: agent capabilities vary significantly and you want tasks assigned to the most capable available agent, you need to load balance across agents with varying workloads, or you want to allow agents to specialize dynamically based on demand.

The implementation requires: a task queue where tasks are posted, a bidding mechanism where agents submit bids (which might include a capability estimate and a cost estimate), and an auction mechanism that assigns tasks based on bids.

Market-based coordination adds significant overhead compared to direct delegation and is harder to debug (understanding why a specific agent was assigned a specific task requires looking at the bidding history). It's justified only when the dynamic allocation benefits outweigh the overhead.

Consensus Protocols

For decisions that affect multiple agents or that require collective agreement, consensus protocols provide structured mechanisms for reaching agreement.

Simple majority voting works for classification tasks where multiple agents independently assess the same input. Each agent provides its classification, and the majority view is taken as the system's output. This is robust to individual agent errors but requires all agents to be asked about every input, which is expensive.

Weighted voting gives different agents different influence based on their historical accuracy on similar tasks. An agent that has been highly accurate on a specific type of task gets more influence on that task type. This requires tracking per-agent accuracy by task type, which adds operational overhead but produces better outcomes than uniform weighting.

Delphi-style consensus iterates through multiple rounds of assessment, where each agent's response in each round is informed by the responses of other agents in the previous round. This allows agents to update their assessments based on new information without fully deferring to each other. It's slower than one-round voting but tends to produce better-calibrated outputs for complex judgment tasks.

Chapter 13 Extended: Building Evaluation Systems That Scale

Automated Evaluation at Scale

For high-volume agentic systems, manual evaluation of outputs is not feasible for routine monitoring. Building automated evaluation pipelines that run continuously without human intervention is necessary.

Rule-based checks are the cheapest form of automated evaluation and should be applied first. Does the output meet format requirements? Is it within the expected length range? Does it contain required elements? Does it avoid prohibited elements? These checks are deterministic and fast.

Semantic similarity checks compare outputs to reference examples using embeddings. If an output is semantically similar to high-quality reference examples and dissimilar to low-quality examples, it's likely (but not certain) to be good. This is faster and cheaper than LLM-as-judge but less accurate.

LLM-as-judge is the most accurate automated evaluation approach but also the most expensive. Use it selectively: for a random sample of outputs to monitor quality trends, for outputs that rule-based and similarity checks flag as potentially problematic, and for periodic comprehensive audits.

Combining these layers, with rule-based checks running on everything, similarity checks running on a larger sample, and LLM-as-judge on a smaller sample, provides continuous quality monitoring at reasonable cost.

Evaluation Metrics That Actually Matter

A failure mode in agentic system evaluation is optimizing for metrics that are easy to measure rather than metrics that reflect what actually matters to users.

Task completion rate sounds like a good metric until you realize that a system can achieve high completion rates by producing outputs that technically complete the task while being useless. "Completed" should mean "completed correctly and usefully," which requires either subjective human evaluation or more specific objective criteria.

User satisfaction metrics (explicit ratings, implicit signals like repeat usage, time spent with outputs) are harder to collect but more directly connected to actual value. Building mechanisms to collect these signals early in deployment is worth the effort.

Business outcome metrics, when you can link them to agent behavior, are the most meaningful evaluation. Did the research assistant's output actually help the analyst write a better report? Did the customer service agent actually resolve the customer's problem? These metrics require connecting agent behavior to downstream outcomes, which is a non-trivial instrumentation challenge.

Evaluating Novel Cases

Evaluation is most valuable for the cases you haven't anticipated. Novel cases, situations that are outside the distribution of what you designed and tested for, are where most production failures occur.

Building a "novelty detector" that flags inputs that are significantly different from the training distribution is one approach. Novel cases can be routed for human evaluation before being processed, or processed with extra caution and flagged for review after.

Analyzing failure cases from production for common patterns is another approach. When the system fails in similar ways repeatedly, that pattern reveals a systematic gap in the design. Incorporating examples of this gap into the evaluation set and addressing the underlying cause improves performance on the whole class of similar cases.

Chapter 14 Extended: Human Oversight in Practice

Designing Effective Review Interfaces

When the system involves a human reviewer, the interface through which they review is as important as the content being reviewed. A well-designed review interface makes the reviewer's job easier and produces better decisions.

Context presentation: the reviewer needs enough context to make a good decision without being overwhelmed. Design the interface to show the most important context prominently and make additional context available on request rather than showing everything by default.

Decision framing: present the reviewer with a clear, specific decision to make rather than asking them to assess the situation generally. "Should this email be sent as written, revised, or held for further review?" is more actionable than "please review this email."

Option provision: give reviewers the tools to implement their decision efficiently. If they approve with minor changes, they should be able to make those changes directly in the interface rather than having to go through a separate editing process.

Time awareness: some review decisions are time-sensitive and some are not. The interface should clearly communicate urgency, and the workflow should allow reviewers to prioritize appropriately.

Asynchronous vs Synchronous Review

Some review workflows are synchronous: the system waits for reviewer input before proceeding. Others are asynchronous: the system continues working and the reviewer's input is incorporated when available.

Synchronous review is appropriate when: the reviewer's decision affects the current action (approve before sending), the decision is time-sensitive and waiting is acceptable, or the cost of proceeding incorrectly is very high.

Asynchronous review is appropriate when: the system can make progress on other aspects of the task while waiting for review, the reviewer's input improves future outputs but isn't required for current ones, or the review volume is high enough that synchronous review would create unacceptable bottlenecks.

Hybrid approaches, where the system proceeds with a best-effort output but incorporates review feedback when it arrives to improve future outputs, work well for recommendation and personalization use cases.

Reducing Review Burden Over Time

The goal of a well-designed human-in-the-loop system is to gradually reduce the review burden as confidence in the system builds, while maintaining the ability to increase oversight when problems are detected.

Tracking review outcomes systematically, what fraction of items are approved unchanged, what fraction are approved with modifications, what fraction are rejected, allows identification of the cases where review adds the most value and those where it adds the least.

Cases where items are consistently approved unchanged are candidates for removing review. Cases where items are consistently rejected or require significant modification identify systematic problems in the system that are better addressed by improving the system than by continuing to rely on human correction.

Maintaining a "review on demand" capability, where users can request review for cases that seem uncertain even when routine review has been removed, preserves the safety net while reducing routine overhead.

Chapter 15 Extended: Governance Frameworks and Compliance

Building a Governance Framework

A governance framework for an agentic system is a documented set of policies, procedures, and controls that define how the system is operated, monitored, and maintained.

The key components of an effective framework:

System purpose statement: a clear description of what the system is designed to do and, importantly, what it is not designed to do. This scoping document is the reference point for all other governance decisions.

Authorization model: who is authorized to use the system, for what purposes, with what permissions. This might map directly to organizational roles or might involve purpose-specific access controls.

Action classification: every action the system can take, classified by its risk level, reversibility, and authorization requirements. This is the governance document that most directly affects system behavior.

Escalation procedures: specific, testable procedures for each type of escalation the system might trigger. "Escalate to a human when uncertain" is not a procedure; "send an alert to the designated reviewer at [address] with the context information in [format] and wait up to [time limit] for a response before defaulting to [fallback action]" is a procedure.

Incident response plan: documented procedures for different types of incidents, including who to notify, what immediate actions to take, and how to conduct a root cause analysis.

Review schedule: when each component of the governance framework is reviewed and updated. Governance frameworks that are never updated become irrelevant.

Regulatory Compliance Considerations

Different industries have different regulatory requirements for automated systems, and agentic systems often have more exposure to these requirements than simpler LLM applications because they take real-world actions.

Healthcare: AI systems that interact with patient data or influence clinical decisions may be subject to HIPAA, FDA medical device regulations, and various state-level regulations. The patient navigation case study in the previous chapter required significant legal review before deployment.

Financial services: AI systems that provide advice, execute transactions, or access financial data may be subject to SEC, FINRA, and various banking regulations. The research copilot case study required compliance review to ensure it wasn't providing regulated investment advice.

Legal: AI systems used in legal work face unauthorized practice of law concerns if they provide legal advice. The legal brief assistant case study was carefully designed as an assistant tool, not as an autonomous legal advisor, specifically to avoid this issue.

Privacy: systems that process personal data may be subject to GDPR, CCPA, or other privacy regulations. The key requirements are typically: consent for data processing, purpose limitation, data minimization, retention limits, and rights to access and deletion.

Getting appropriate legal review for the specific regulatory context your system operates in is strongly advisable. What counts as "providing advice," "making a decision," or "processing personal data" varies by jurisdiction and by the specific facts of the situation.

Building for Auditability

Regulatory compliance often requires demonstrating that systems behave consistently with documented policies and that you know what actions were taken and why.

Complete audit trails: every action the system takes should be logged with: who authorized the action (user, agent, or automated rule), what the action was, what inputs led to the decision to take it, what the outcome was, and when each step happened.

Decision explanations: for systems that make significant decisions, the ability to explain why a specific decision was made may be required. This is different from interpretability of the underlying model; it's about reconstructing the specific reasoning path that led to a specific decision for a specific input.

Policy enforcement documentation: records showing that policy rules were checked and either passed or triggered escalation for every action covered by those rules. This demonstrates that controls are actually being enforced, not just described.

Data lineage: for systems that process and transform data, tracking what data was used for each output, where it came from, and what transformations were applied. This is particularly important for systems in regulated data environments.

Chapter 6 Final Content: CWD Anti-Patterns

Learning what not to do is often as useful as learning what to do. Several CWD anti-patterns come up repeatedly in systems I've reviewed.

The monolithic coordinator anti-pattern: the coordinator tries to do too much. It generates the plan, routes tasks, evaluates outputs, and handles failures. This makes the coordinator prompt enormous, brittle, and difficult to debug. When something goes wrong, you don't know which of the coordinator's responsibilities failed.

Fix: split the coordinator into at least two components: one that generates and revises the plan (the planner) and one that routes tasks and handles failures (the orchestrator). These have different capabilities and different failure modes, and separating them makes both easier to optimize.

The homogeneous workers anti-pattern: all workers are identical instances of the same prompt. This eliminates the specialization benefit of the CWD pattern.

Fix: give each worker a genuinely different prompt optimized for its specific task type. A research worker prompt should be designed around research tasks; a writing worker prompt around writing tasks. They should share a common interface (same input format, same output format) but different task-specific instructions.

The stateless coordinator anti-pattern: the coordinator doesn't maintain state between calls and has to re-infer the current situation from the accumulated outputs each time. This is inefficient and error-prone, particularly for long tasks.

Fix: maintain explicit state between coordinator calls. Track which tasks are complete, what their outputs were, and what the next planned steps are. Inject this state into each coordinator call rather than asking the coordinator to infer it.

The over-delegated anti-pattern: tasks are broken into such small pieces that the coordination overhead exceeds the work being done. The coordinator spends more time managing subtasks than the workers spend executing them.

Fix: balance decomposition depth against coordination overhead. A good heuristic: if a worker could complete the task in a single call, it probably doesn't need to be further decomposed. If completing a task would require more than five or six tool calls, it might benefit from further decomposition.

Chapter 7 Final Content: Reactive Agent Design Patterns

Input Normalization

Before a reactive agent processes input, normalizing it reduces the variation the agent has to handle. Normalization might include: standardizing text casing, removing extra whitespace, resolving abbreviations and synonyms, converting dates and numbers to standard formats.

The value of normalization: it means inputs that mean the same thing but look different (customer vs. cust. vs. Customer) are treated identically, reducing the variation that the agent's logic has to handle and making evaluation more reliable.

Output Standardization

Symmetric to input normalization, output standardization ensures that the agent's output is always in a predictable format. Even when the downstream consumer is flexible, standardized outputs are easier to log, easier to monitor, and easier to hand off to other components.

Define output schemas explicitly, not just as documentation but as validation schemas that are checked on every output. Schema validation at the output layer catches format errors before they propagate downstream.

Chapter 8 Final Content: Planning Under Uncertainty

Plans fail when assumptions turn out to be wrong. A plan that says "retrieve data from source X, then analyze it" assumes source X will be available and will return useful data. If either assumption is wrong, the plan needs to be revised.

Building uncertainty explicitly into plans is one of the most useful practices for making deliberative agents more reliable. For each step in a plan, specify: what assumptions does this step make? What happens if those assumptions are wrong? What's the fallback?

This isn't just documentation; it changes how the agent executes. When the agent can refer to explicitly stated fallback plans for each step, it doesn't need to reason about what to do when something fails; the fallback is already specified. This makes failure handling faster and more consistent.

Conditional planning is a more formal version of this: instead of a single linear plan, generate a branching plan where different branches are followed based on what actually happens. The plan is more complex but more robust, because failure paths are explicit rather than discovered at runtime.

Chapter 9 Final Content: Hybrid System Monitoring

Monitoring a hybrid system requires separate instrumentation for the routing layer and for each of the reactive and deliberative paths.

The routing layer produces a stream of routing decisions: this request went to reactive, this one went to deliberative. Monitoring the distribution of these decisions over time tells you whether the distribution is shifting (which would suggest a change in the input distribution that might require rebalancing the routing thresholds).

The reactive path has its own quality metrics: accuracy rate, latency, cost. If any of these degrade, it's a signal that either the input distribution has shifted or the reactive agent needs updating.

The deliberative path's metrics: task completion rate, output quality, latency, cost per task. Higher costs and latencies are expected and acceptable for deliberative processing; the question is whether they're producing proportionately better outcomes.

The overall system metrics: what's the end-to-end accuracy? What's the end-to-end latency distribution? What's the cost per user request? These tell you whether the hybrid architecture is achieving its goal of better outcomes at better economics than a purely reactive or purely deliberative system.

Chapter 10 Final Content: Tool Failure Analysis

When tools fail, understanding why they failed is essential for improving system reliability.

Failure taxonomy: tool failures typically fall into several categories. Network failures (the service is unreachable), authentication failures (credentials are wrong or expired), rate limit failures (too many calls in a time window), input validation failures (the parameters don't meet requirements), service errors (the service is reachable but returns an error), and empty results (the service responds successfully but returns no data).

Each failure type suggests a different response. Network failures are often transient and benefit from retry with backoff. Authentication failures need immediate attention (credentials need to be refreshed or updated). Rate limit failures require either slowing down or switching to an alternative. Input validation failures indicate a model error in parameter generation that should be logged and fed back. Service errors may be transient or permanent and need case-by-case handling. Empty results may be correct (no data matching the query exists) or an error (the query was malformed).

Building explicit handling for each failure type, rather than treating all failures identically, produces much more reliable and informative behavior.

Chapter 11 Final Content: Memory Security Considerations

Memory systems store sensitive information, and securing that information requires deliberate design.

Encryption at rest: data stored in memory systems, particularly user-specific information, should be encrypted. Most managed cloud databases provide this by default; for self-hosted systems, it requires explicit configuration.

Access control: memory retrieval should be scoped to the current user and session. Implementing row-level security or query-level filtering to ensure that each request can only retrieve its own data is essential for multi-user systems.

Data retention policies: memory systems accumulate data over time. Implementing policies that automatically delete data after a defined retention period, rather than storing everything indefinitely, reduces the scope of potential data breaches and ensures compliance with data retention regulations.

Audit logging: access to sensitive memory data should be logged. Who accessed what data, when, and for what purpose. This audit trail is important for both security investigations and regulatory compliance.

Chapter 12 Final Content: Designing for Agent Team Dynamics

Beyond the technical aspects of multi-agent coordination, there are softer design considerations around how agent teams work together.

Role clarity reduces conflict. When each agent has a clear, non-overlapping role, there's less chance that two agents will attempt the same task or produce contradictory outputs. Designing roles to be complementary rather than overlapping is worth the extra thought.

Communication norms affect quality. Agents that communicate verbosely produce context-heavy downstream agents; agents that communicate concisely produce leaner, faster downstream processing. Establishing communication norms (be specific about what you're passing and why, be concise in status reports, be explicit about what you need from the next agent) improves coordination quality.

Failure isolation prevents cascading problems. When one agent fails, that failure shouldn't necessarily stop the whole team. Designing the coordination so that agents can proceed with partial information, flagging what's missing rather than blocking completely, makes the overall system more resilient.

Collective goal alignment ensures agents are working toward the same end. Individual agent goals should be sub-goals of the collective goal, not independent goals that might conflict. A coordinator that maintains the collective goal explicitly and ensures each agent's task contributes to it prevents the goal drift that can occur in complex multi-agent systems.

Chapter 13 Final Content: Evaluation Maturity Model

Teams evaluating agentic systems tend to mature through a progression of evaluation practices.

At the starting level, evaluation is manual and ad-hoc: engineers look at outputs and decide if they're good. This is necessary at the very beginning but doesn't scale.

At the basic level, there's a fixed test set that's run periodically, usually manually or in CI/CD. This catches obvious regressions but provides limited insight into performance on real-world inputs.

At the developing level, evaluation is continuous on production data. Sampling is systematic, metrics are tracked over time, and there's an alerting system for quality degradation. Evaluation results inform improvement decisions.

At the advanced level, evaluation is multi-dimensional and multi-level. Component-level metrics, system-level metrics, and business outcome metrics are tracked. A/B testing infrastructure enables controlled experiments. Evaluation findings drive systematic improvement cycles.

At the mature level, evaluation is proactive as well as reactive. Before releasing changes, their expected impact on evaluation metrics is predicted. Novel failure modes are anticipated and tested for. The evaluation system itself is continuously improved.

Most production teams operate at the developing or advanced level. Getting to the advanced level is within reach with six to twelve months of deliberate investment in evaluation infrastructure.

Chapter 14 Final Content: Organizational Considerations for Human-in-the-Loop

Designing the technical interface between humans and agents is only part of the challenge. There are organizational considerations that significantly affect whether human-in-the-loop works well in practice.

Reviewer capacity: if the system escalates more tasks than reviewers have capacity to handle, the review queue backs up and either the escalated tasks wait too long or reviewers rush through reviews without giving them adequate attention. Right-sizing the review capacity to the expected escalation volume is a logistics challenge that needs to be solved before deployment.

Reviewer quality: reviewers need to know enough about the task domain to make good decisions. A reviewer who doesn't understand the domain will either approve everything (defeating the purpose of review) or flag everything (creating too much back-and-forth). Reviewer training and quality monitoring are important operational practices.

Incentive alignment: reviewers have an easier time when they approve tasks than when they request revisions, because revision creates more work. If reviewer incentives are aligned with throughput rather than quality, approval rates will be too high. Building quality metrics for reviewers alongside throughput metrics helps align incentives with the goal.

Review fatigue: for sustained operations, human reviewers doing the same review task repeatedly will become less attentive over time. Building in variety, rotation across reviewers, and regular breaks for high-volume review operations helps maintain quality.

Chapter 15 Final Content: The Future of AI Governance

Current governance frameworks for AI are still immature relative to the risks. This is acknowledged broadly in the field, including by the major AI providers and by many of the people building these systems.

What we can see coming: regulatory requirements for AI systems in high-stakes domains will tighten. Documentation requirements, testing requirements, incident reporting requirements, and transparency requirements are all areas where regulation is moving in the direction of more rigor. Building governance infrastructure now that can satisfy these requirements when they arrive is smart operational planning.

What's less clear: how liability for AI-caused harms will be allocated. The current state of legal ambiguity will eventually resolve, and the resolution will likely assign more liability to deployers and developers than the current informal norms suggest. Operating as if you're accountable for your system's harms, even when the legal framework doesn't yet require it, is both ethically right and practically prudent.

What will remain constant: the need for systems to be accountable, observable, and improvable. Regardless of how specific regulations evolve, systems that can explain their behavior, that can be audited, and that can be improved when problems are found will be better positioned than those that cannot.

SECTION IV: Applied Agentic Design

Chapter 16

Case Studies and Design Canvases

There is a specific kind of humility that comes from deploying an agentic system into production. Everything that looked clean in the design phase develops edges. Users do things you did not anticipate. APIs that worked in testing fail under load. Memory systems that retrieved well on your evaluation set return irrelevant context on real queries. The governance rules you wrote cover eighty percent of cases and the other twenty percent are more interesting than you expected.

This chapter is about what building and deploying these systems actually looks like. The case studies here are drawn from real production deployments: an e-commerce marketing coordinator, a financial research copilot, a patient navigation system for healthcare, a DevOps automation agent, and several others. Each is examined not as a success story but as an architecture, with its components, its failure modes, and the decisions that were made along the way.

The design canvases at the end of the chapter give you a template structure you can adapt. They are not blueprints to copy; the specific circumstances of your domain will require different choices. They are frameworks for asking the right questions before you build.

Why Real Case Studies Matter

There's a specific genre of AI case study that I find mostly useless: the one that describes what a system does, lists impressive metrics, and moves on. These tell you that a system was built and worked. They don't tell you what was hard, what failed, what was rebuilt, or what decisions the team wishes they had made differently.

The case studies in this chapter try to be more honest than that. They include the things that went wrong, the design decisions that turned out to be mistakes, and the lessons that only became visible after the system was deployed. This kind of detail is what actually helps when you're building something similar.

I've also tried to be specific about the architectural decisions, not just the capabilities. What memory architecture was used and why? How were escalation thresholds set? What did the governance rules actually say? These specifics are more useful than general descriptions of what the system could do.

Case Study 1: AI Marketing Coordinator

An e-commerce brand was running three to five campaigns per week with a small marketing team. The bottleneck was coordination: content writers, ad teams, and product managers were all working from slightly different briefs, producing messaging that was inconsistent and required significant manual reconciliation before campaigns could launch.

The System Architecture

The system used the CWD pattern with four main components.

The coordinator agent read weekly business goals from a structured input (sales targets, promotion priorities, inventory flags) and generated a campaign blueprint specifying what content was needed across channels. It produced a structured JSON plan with explicit tasks for each worker, expected output formats, and deadlines.

Specialist worker agents handled content generation for specific channels: an email agent that wrote subject lines and promotional sequences, an ad agent that created Facebook and Google ad copy variants, and a page agent that updated product page CTAs and hero copy. Each worker was given only the context it needed for its specific task, not the full campaign brief.

A critic agent reviewed all outputs before anything went to human approval. It checked for tone consistency, policy compliance, and flagged outputs that fell outside confidence thresholds. The critic's rubric was defined by the marketing team and updated monthly based on what had been approved versus rejected.

The memory layer stored prior campaign performance data linked to the creative choices that produced those outcomes. It also maintained a running model of the brand voice, updated after each campaign based on what the human reviewers approved versus revised.

What Worked

The separation between the coordinator and the workers was the most valuable architectural decision. When a worker produced poor output, the problem was isolated to that worker's prompt and context, not to the coordinator or the critic. When the overall campaign strategy was wrong, the problem was isolated to the coordinator. This made debugging and improvement much faster than a monolithic system would have.

The critic agent initially seemed like overhead. In practice, it caught a significant fraction of policy violations and tone inconsistencies before they reached human reviewers, which reduced the review burden substantially. The catch: the critic's rubric needed to be much more specific than the team initially expected. "Check for brand tone consistency" is too vague. "Flag any instance of informal contractions, first-person plural, or price-specific claims that don't match the current promotion schedule" is actionable.

What Failed

The memory system's initial design stored campaign outcomes at the campaign level, which was too coarse. Two campaigns might have similar overall performance but very different performance across channels, and the memory system couldn't distinguish them. Changing to channel-level outcome storage improved the relevance of retrieved memories significantly.

The governance rules initially required human approval for all content. This was appropriate at launch but created a bottleneck once the team gained confidence in the system. Implementing a tiered approval system, where low-impact content (internal newsletters, social posts under a budget threshold) was published automatically and higher-impact content required approval, doubled throughput without a measurable quality decrease.

The most unexpected failure: the coordinator occasionally generated campaigns that were internally consistent but completely wrong for the current business situation. An inventory shortage of a promoted product, a pending price change, a PR situation requiring tone adjustment: the coordinator had no visibility into these unless they were explicitly encoded in the input. Building a more comprehensive "current context" input that included operational flags beyond just sales targets fixed most of these cases.

Lessons

Modularity matters more for debugging than for initial development. The initial development of a monolithic agent might have been faster. The debugging and iteration benefits of the modular design appeared over the following months.

Governance needs to evolve with confidence. Starting conservative and relaxing constraints based on observed performance is much safer than starting permissive and trying to tighten constraints after problems occur.

Memory at the right granularity is as important as memory at all. Coarse-grained memory that stored campaign-level performance was worse than no memory in some cases, because it retrieved misleading context.

Case Study 2: Research Copilot for Financial Analysts

Analysts at a mid-sized research firm were spending roughly sixty percent of their time on tasks that were not core to decision-making: searching for sources, summarizing documents, reformatting findings for different audiences.

The System Architecture

The deliberative core accepted natural language goal statements and decomposed them into subtasks: identifying relevant sources, retrieving and summarizing those sources, synthesizing the findings, and formatting the output to the analyst's preferred style.

The retrieval agent connected to internal knowledge bases, licensed data providers (Bloomberg, Gartner, McKinsey reports), and the web through custom scrapers. It maintained a source quality model that weighted sources by reliability and recency.

A summarizer agent adapted outputs to the individual analyst's style preferences, which were stored in the memory layer and updated based on feedback. The memory layer tracked per-user style preferences, past report topics and client-specific nuances, and a terminology dictionary for industry or firm-specific language.

A feedback loop collected ratings after each delivery on relevance, clarity, and accuracy. These ratings updated the retrieval weighting and summarization style for that analyst's future sessions.

The Personalization Challenge

The most technically interesting part of this system was the personalization layer. Different analysts had substantially different preferences: some wanted dense bullet points, others wanted narrative prose. Some wanted sources cited inline, others at the end. Some were generalists who needed more context, others were specialists who needed less.

The initial approach to personalization was to ask analysts to fill out a preference survey at onboarding. This worked poorly. Survey responses didn't capture the nuances of what analysts actually wanted, and preferences changed over time.

The approach that worked better was implicit feedback collection. After each report delivery, the system logged: did the analyst use the report directly or request revisions? If they requested revisions, what kind? Did they copy-paste sections or regenerate them? Over a few weeks of use, these implicit signals produced a much richer model of each analyst's preferences than the explicit survey had.

The privacy implication of storing detailed preference models per analyst required explicit handling. Analysts were informed what was stored, could review and delete their preference data, and could opt out of personalization entirely.

What Failed Initially

The retrieval agent's initial source quality model was too static. It weighted sources based on domain reputation (Bloomberg rated highly, random blogs rated low) without accounting for how relevant a specific source was to the specific query. A highly reputable source that covered a different market segment was being retrieved over a less reputable source that was directly relevant.

Adding query-specific relevance scoring, which weighted sources by both general quality and specific relevance to the current query, improved retrieval quality substantially.

The summarization agent initially produced outputs that were too long for most use cases. Analysts wanted briefings, not comprehensive summaries. Calibrating the target length to the complexity of the query, not to the length of the source material, produced much more usable outputs.

Lessons

Implicit feedback is richer than explicit surveys for personalization, but requires more careful privacy handling.

Source quality and query relevance are independent dimensions. Systems that conflate them tend to retrieve highly reputable but irrelevant sources.

Output length calibration matters as much as output quality. A perfect summary that's three times longer than the user wants is still frustrating.

Case Study 3: Patient Navigator in Healthcare

A hospital system was seeing patients fall through the cracks during care transitions: patients discharged from one department who did not follow up with the next provider, patients who did not understand their care instructions, patients who were not getting the preventive care their condition warranted.

The patient navigator agent was built to maintain continuity across those transitions. It had access to the electronic medical record, the appointment scheduling system, and a messaging platform for patient communication.

The Scope Problem

Defining the scope of what the agent would and would not address was the central design challenge. Healthcare is a domain where the cost of getting it wrong is very high.

The team approached this by defining an explicit inclusion list (the agent would address appointment scheduling questions, general care plan reminders, navigation to appropriate resources) and an explicit exclusion list (the agent would not address symptoms, diagnoses, medication questions, or anything requiring clinical judgment). The exclusion list was developed collaboratively with clinical staff and reviewed by the hospital's medical director.

The agent was given a very conservative uncertainty threshold: if it was not highly confident that a question fell within its scope, it escalated to clinical staff. The false positive rate for escalation was intentionally high at launch, with the plan to calibrate it downward based on observed performance.

What surprised the team was how often patients asked questions that were adjacent to but outside the agent's scope. A patient asking "what foods should I avoid with my new medication" is asking a dietary question (potentially in scope) and a medication question (out of scope). The agent's initial response to these mixed questions was inconsistent. Building explicit handling for questions that crossed scope boundaries, routing them to clinical staff with a summary of what the patient had asked, resolved most of these cases.

Privacy Architecture

The privacy architecture required more careful design than almost any other aspect of the system.

The agent was given access only to the data it needed for its specific function: the patient's upcoming appointments, their care plan summary, and their communication history with the navigator. It did not have access to full medical records, billing information, or historical records from before the current care episode.

Every patient interaction was logged to the medical record as a clinical note, making it subject to standard clinical documentation standards and auditing. This was both a compliance requirement and a practical benefit: it gave clinical staff visibility into what patients had been told, which reduced confusion during follow-up appointments.

Case Study 4: DevOps Automation Agent

A software engineering organization was dealing with a common operational problem: incident response required significant manual work to diagnose, coordinate, and resolve, pulling engineers away from development work and creating bottlenecks during high-stress situations.

The DevOps automation agent was built to handle first-response for incidents.

The Reversibility Taxonomy

The most important design decision in this system was the reversibility classification for all actions in the agent's scope.

Every action was tagged as one of three categories. Read-only actions (querying logs, retrieving metrics, generating reports) could be executed automatically with no approval. Reversible actions (restarting a service, clearing a cache, scaling a resource up) required logging and could be executed automatically if the agent's confidence exceeded a threshold. Irreversible actions (deleting data, modifying database schemas, infrastructure changes with dependencies) required explicit human approval regardless of confidence level.

This classification was maintained as a separate document, reviewed by the engineering team quarterly, and updated when new tools were added to the agent's scope. The taxonomy itself was valuable beyond the agent: it prompted the team to think carefully about the operational properties of each of their tools in a way they hadn't before.

What Failed Initially

The incident knowledge base was initially organized by incident type (database, networking, application) which matched how incidents were categorized but not how they were diagnosed. When the agent received an alert, it needed to retrieve similar past incidents, but "similar" in diagnostic terms often cut across incident types.

Reorganizing the knowledge base around symptom patterns rather than incident categories, and updating the retrieval strategy accordingly, improved the agent's diagnosis quality substantially.

The confidence thresholds for automatic reversible actions were initially set too conservatively. The agent was escalating cases to engineers that it was handling correctly, which increased the number of interruptions rather than reducing them. Empirically calibrating the thresholds against observed outcomes over six weeks allowed reducing the escalation rate significantly while maintaining quality.

Case Study 5: E-Commerce Growth Strategist

A direct-to-consumer brand wanted to identify growth opportunities across their product catalog and customer segments more systematically than their small team could manage manually.

The Goal Decomposition Challenge

"Identify growth opportunities" is not a specific enough goal for a planning agent to work with. The design process involved working with the business team to decompose that high-level goal into specific analytical questions: which customer segments have the highest unmet demand? Which products have the highest return rates and why? Where does the conversion funnel lose customers for which product categories?

Each question had a defined analytical approach and a defined output format. This decomposition work, taking a vague business objective and turning it into specific, evaluable analytical tasks, was as valuable as the agent itself. Several of the analytical approaches the team defined became manual processes before they became automated ones, because the work of definition revealed gaps in data availability and organizational readiness.

The lesson: the work of translating a business goal into a specific enough representation that an agent can pursue it systematically is itself valuable, separate from whether you build an agent to pursue it.

Case Study 6: Legal Brief Assistant

A mid-sized law firm built an agent to assist associates with legal research and initial brief drafting. This case is worth examining in detail because the governance requirements were more stringent than in most domains.

The system was designed explicitly as an assistant, not as an autonomous agent. Every output carried a prominent disclaimer that it was AI-generated and required attorney review before use. The system could not file anything, send anything, or take any action that had legal significance; it could only produce draft documents for human review.

The verification architecture was particularly interesting. For every factual claim in a generated brief, the system produced an annotation linking the claim to the source it came from. Attorneys could see exactly where each claim originated and verify it directly. Claims for which no reliable source could be found were flagged rather than omitted, so attorneys knew what was unverified rather than assuming everything was verified.

This verification architecture turned out to be the most valuable feature of the system. Attorneys reported that it changed how they interacted with the output: rather than reviewing it as a draft to correct, they used it as a structured research summary that they could verify and build on. The agent's value was primarily in organizing and presenting information, not in the quality of its prose.

Design Canvases

The following canvases provide a starting point for designing agentic systems in specific contexts. Each canvas has the same structure: the goal, the agent components, the memory design, the tool interfaces, the governance rules, and the key questions to answer before building.

AI Marketing Coordinator Canvas

Goal: coordinate multi-channel campaign production with consistent brand voice and measurable performance tracking.

Core agents: coordinator (plans campaigns, assigns tasks), specialist workers (channel-specific content generation), critic (quality and compliance review).

Memory: campaign performance history linked to creative decisions; brand voice model updated from human feedback; promotional calendar and inventory state.

Tools: CMS integration, email platform, ad platform, analytics platform.

Governance: human approval required for all external-facing content above a defined impact threshold; budget controls enforced at tool interface; all actions logged.

Key questions: What is the impact threshold for requiring human approval? How is brand voice defined and who owns updates to it? What happens when the coordinator and critic disagree? How does the memory system handle seasonal patterns that shouldn't be applied year-round?

Research Copilot Canvas

Goal: reduce time analysts spend on information gathering and formatting without reducing the quality of their judgment on the findings.

Core agents: planner (decomposes research goals), retrieval (sources documents), summarizer (adapts to user style), reviewer (checks source attribution).

Memory: per-user style preferences and feedback history; organizational knowledge base; source quality ratings.

Tools: licensed data feeds, internal document stores, web scraping.

Governance: all factual claims require source attribution; no client-facing output without human approval; data access limited to what the analyst's role permits.

Key questions: How is source quality evaluated? What happens when the system cannot find sufficient sources? How is feedback collected without creating friction that discourages use? How is the personalization model updated when user preferences change?

Patient Navigation Canvas

Goal: maintain care plan continuity for patients across care transitions.

Core agents: care coordinator (tracks care plan status, identifies gaps), communicator (patient-facing messaging within defined scope), escalation handler (routes out-of-scope interactions to clinical staff).

Memory: patient care plan state; interaction history; escalation log.

Tools: EHR read access, scheduling system, patient messaging platform.

Governance: conservative uncertainty threshold for escalation to clinical staff; strict scope boundary maintained and reviewed quarterly; all interactions logged to medical record; clinical review of all escalation decisions.

Key questions: How is the scope boundary maintained and updated? Who reviews escalations and on what timeline? What are the privacy requirements and how are they enforced architecturally? How does the system handle patients who are confused or distressed?

DevOps Automation Canvas

Goal: reduce mean time to resolution for infrastructure incidents by automating first-response diagnosis and low-risk remediation.

Core agents: alert classifier (reactive, categorizes incoming alerts), diagnostic agent (deliberative, characterizes the incident), remediation planner (selects response approach), executor (takes actions within defined scope).

Memory: incident history indexed by symptom patterns; runbook knowledge base; reversibility classification for all actions.

Tools: monitoring systems, log aggregation, infrastructure management APIs, incident communication platform.

Governance: reversibility classification required for all actions; irreversible actions require human approval regardless of confidence; all actions logged with rationale; on-call engineer receives structured briefing for all incidents.

Key questions: How is the reversibility classification maintained as the system's action scope evolves? How is the incident knowledge base updated with new cases? What triggers an escalation during automated remediation? How are false positive escalations tracked and used to calibrate thresholds?

Legal Research Assistant Canvas

Goal: reduce time associates spend on legal research while maintaining the accuracy and source traceability required for legal work.

Core agents: researcher (finds and retrieves relevant cases, statutes, and commentary), synthesizer (organizes findings into structured summaries), drafter (produces initial brief sections), verifier (checks claims against sources).

Memory: matter-specific context; citation database; attorney style preferences.

Tools: legal research databases (Westlaw, LexisNexis), internal document store, citation checker.

Governance: all outputs carry AI-generated disclaimer; no output used in filed documents without attorney review; all factual claims linked to verifiable sources; no autonomous communication with clients or opposing counsel.

Key questions: How are claims that cannot be sourced handled? What level of attorney review is required before output is used? How is the system updated when law changes? How are hallucinated citations detected and prevented?

E-Commerce Growth Strategist Canvas

Goal: identify and prioritize growth opportunities across product catalog and customer segments.

Core agents: data retriever (pulls relevant sales, returns, and engagement data), analyst (identifies patterns and anomalies), hypothesis generator (produces prioritized opportunity list), validator (checks hypotheses against additional data).

Memory: historical opportunity assessments and outcomes; seasonal patterns; team priorities and constraints.

Tools: analytics platform, CRM, A/B testing platform, financial modeling tools.

Governance: all recommendations require human review before action; no direct access to production systems; recommendations include confidence levels and key assumptions.

Key questions: How are business constraints and priorities communicated to the system? How are the outcomes of implemented recommendations tracked back to the system's suggestions? How does the system handle situations where data quality is poor?

CONCLUSION

I want to end with something honest about where the field is right now, because I think the books in this space tend toward either uncritical enthusiasm or exaggerated caution, and neither is useful.

The systems described in this book work. They produce real value in production, for organizations that have built them thoughtfully and invested in the operational practices required to maintain them. The case studies in the previous chapter are not exceptional outcomes; they are representative of what teams with reasonable engineering capability can achieve with current tools and techniques.

The systems described in this book also fail, regularly, in ways that require ongoing attention to catch and correct. Memory systems drift. Models change behavior when providers update them. User behavior evolves in ways that break assumptions baked into the design. Governance rules that covered the original use case do not cover the use case as it has evolved.

Looking Back at the Common Thread

The most consistent theme across the case studies is that the hard problems were almost never the ones that seemed hard at the start. The language model capabilities were mostly adequate. The frameworks largely did what they promised. What took the most work was the surrounding infrastructure: the memory architecture, the governance rules, the evaluation systems, the escalation paths, the feedback loops.

Teams that invested in this surrounding infrastructure early built systems that improved steadily over time and held up under real conditions. Teams that treated infrastructure as something to add later spent most of their time firefighting problems that could have been avoided.

This is not a unique observation about agentic AI. It's the same lesson that software engineering has learned repeatedly across many paradigms: the code that does the thing is often the easy part. The code that makes the thing reliable, observable, and maintainable is where the real work is.

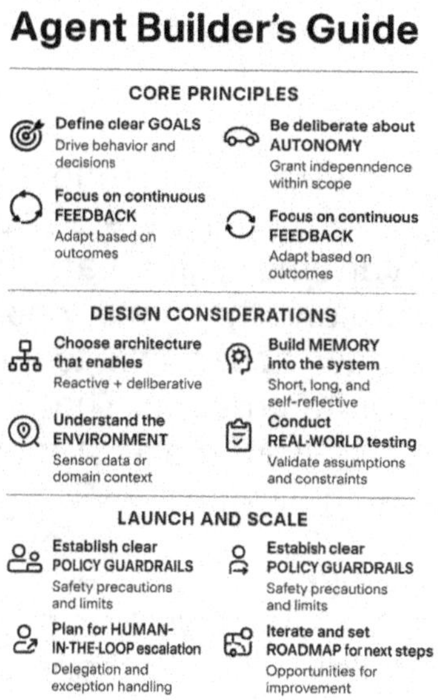

The Oversight Question

I want to say something direct about human oversight, because I've seen it treated as a temporary limitation that will go away as models improve. I don't think that's right.

The need for human oversight in agentic systems is not primarily a matter of model capability. It's a matter of accountability, of having humans who are responsible for the consequences of actions that affect other humans. That need doesn't diminish as models get more capable; it becomes more important, because the consequences of the actions being taken become larger.

This doesn't mean every action requires human approval. It means that the systems taking consequential autonomous actions need to be designed and operated by people who take responsibility for those actions, who monitor them, who can and do intervene when things go wrong. The oversight might be asynchronous, might be statistical rather than comprehensive, but it should be real.

What's Actually New

Something genuinely new has happened with the current generation of language models: the ability to build systems that pursue goals over time, using natural language as both the control mechanism and the primary output, with access to real-world tools, is now accessible to practitioners without specialized research infrastructure. That is a real change. The tools and frameworks that make it possible are mature enough to build real things with.

What has not changed: the fundamental engineering challenges of building reliable systems that operate in the real world. Memory fails. APIs change. Users behave unexpectedly. Requirements evolve. These challenges apply to agentic systems as much as to any other kind of software, and they don't get easier because the underlying model is more capable.

The practitioners who will do the most valuable work in this space are, I think, the ones who hold both of these things at once: genuine enthusiasm for what is now possible, and genuine seriousness about the operational requirements for making it work well. The architecture, the memory design, the tool integration, the evaluation infrastructure, the governance framework, the escalation paths: these are not optional additions to an otherwise complete system. They are the system, as much as the model is.

I hope the book has been useful. Build something real with it.

Chapter 16 Extended: More Case Studies

Case Study 7: AI-Powered Onboarding System

A technology company with rapid headcount growth was struggling with new hire onboarding. The existing process required significant time from HR and managers, produced inconsistent outcomes depending on which manager was involved, and left many new hires uncertain about where to find information and who to ask for help.

The onboarding agent was designed to guide new hires through their first 90 days. It had access to the HR information system, the internal knowledge base, the ticketing system for IT requests, and the org chart.

The key design challenge was personalization at scale. Onboarding needs are different for different roles, different levels of seniority, different teams, and different backgrounds. A one-size-fits-all onboarding sequence produces mediocre outcomes; personalized sequences are much better but require either significant manual work or an intelligent system to generate them.

The agent generated a personalized onboarding plan for each new hire based on their role, team, and background, drawing on templates defined by HR and customized based on input from the hiring manager. The plan specified tasks to complete, people to meet, documents to read, and questions to ask, sequenced appropriately for the first 30, 60, and 90 days.

The agent then actively guided the new hire through the plan: sending reminders, answering questions, booking meetings with the right people, and surfacing relevant resources at the right time. When it encountered questions it couldn't answer, it identified the right person to ask and either connected the new hire directly or asked on their behalf.

What worked surprisingly well was the agent's ability to handle the long tail of questions that new hires have but often don't know who to ask. Questions like "is it normal to feel lost in the first few weeks?" or "where do I find the expense reimbursement form?" are easy to answer but time-consuming when multiplied across hundreds of new hires. Routing these to the agent instead of to HR staff freed significant capacity.

What required iteration was the escalation logic for sensitive situations. New hires sometimes share concerns during onboarding that should be treated with care: concerns about their manager's behavior, concerns about team dynamics, personal challenges that are affecting their work. The initial version of the agent handled these poorly, either ignoring them or responding with generic advice. Building explicit handling for sensitive topics, with clear escalation paths to HR business partners, significantly improved outcomes for these cases.

The 90-day retention rate for new hires who went through the AI-assisted onboarding was meaningfully higher than for those who went through the previous process, though attributing this entirely to the onboarding system would be an overstatement since several other changes happened simultaneously.

Case Study 8: Supply Chain Visibility Agent

A manufacturing company with a complex global supply chain was dealing with a recurring problem: by the time they learned about disruptions (supplier delays, shipping problems, quality issues), it was too late to avoid impact on production. The information was available, but it was scattered across systems and nobody was synthesizing it proactively.

The supply chain visibility agent was built to monitor all relevant data sources continuously and alert operations managers when it detected situations that required attention.

The monitoring architecture had three layers. A data collection layer aggregated information from supplier portals, shipping tracking systems, quality management systems, and news feeds covering supply chain disruptions. A detection layer ran continuous analysis looking for patterns that historically preceded problems: lead times extending beyond normal ranges, quality metrics trending in the wrong direction, shipping delays accumulating in specific lanes. An alert layer generated structured alerts when detection thresholds were crossed, summarizing the situation and the potential impact.

The most technically challenging part was calibrating the detection thresholds. Too sensitive and the alert volume overwhelms operations managers, who start ignoring alerts. Too insensitive and the system misses genuine problems. Getting this calibration right required six months of parallel operation, where the agent generated alerts and operations managers rated each alert as genuine or false positive. That feedback allowed iterative threshold refinement.

What the company found after a year of operation was that the agent's value was not primarily in catching dramatic disruptions, which were already being caught by existing processes, but in catching gradual degradations that accumulated slowly enough that no single data point triggered manual review. A supplier's on-time delivery rate declining from 98% to 89% over three months was not visible without the systematic monitoring the agent provided.

Case Study 9: Content Moderation at Scale

A social platform was dealing with the classic content moderation scaling problem: user-generated content was growing faster than the human moderation team could handle, and the backlog of unreviewed content was becoming a liability.

The content moderation agent was designed to handle the first-pass review of all content, either approving it for publication, removing it automatically for clear violations, or routing it to human reviewers for ambiguous cases.

The three-tier design was the most important architectural decision. Tier one handled obvious approvals: content that clearly met all guidelines and had no warning signals. This tier was a fast, cheap reactive classifier. Tier two handled obvious violations: content that clearly violated guidelines on the dimensions that mattered most (explicit violence, illegal content, obvious harassment). This tier was also a reactive classifier, slightly more expensive because the consequences of false positives (removing legitimate content) justified the additional cost. Tier three handled everything else: the ambiguous middle ground that required judgment. This tier used a deliberative agent that considered multiple factors and generated a recommendation with reasoning for human review.

The volume breakdown that emerged: tier one handled about 75% of content, tier two about 5%, tier three about 20%. The 20% routed to human review was carefully designed to be the cases where human judgment genuinely added value. Cases where the outcome was obvious in either direction were handled automatically; cases requiring context, cultural understanding, or difficult tradeoffs went to humans.

The false positive rate for automatic removal was the metric watched most carefully, because removing legitimate content from users who hadn't violated any policy was both a user experience problem and a trust issue. Keeping this rate below 0.1% was a design constraint that shaped the tier two threshold calibration.

Case Study 10: Personalized Learning Agent

An educational platform was trying to address a fundamental challenge in online learning: the same content is appropriate for some learners and wrong for others, but personalizing at scale is difficult.

The personalized learning agent adapted the learning experience for each student based on their demonstrated understanding, learning pace, and areas of difficulty. It monitored engagement and comprehension signals, identified when a student was struggling, and adapted the sequence of content, the level of explanation, and the type of practice exercises accordingly.

The adaptation logic was the most interesting design problem. There are many dimensions along which learning can be personalized: depth of explanation, type of examples (abstract vs concrete), pace of progression, frequency of review, and framing of challenges. The agent learned which combination of adaptations worked for each student based on their engagement and assessment performance.

This required a learning model at the agent level: the agent itself improved its personalization strategy for each student over time. The memory system stored not just what each student had learned but what pedagogical approaches had worked for them and which hadn't.

The most unexpected finding was that the optimal adaptation strategy varied significantly not just across students but for the same student on different topics. A student who responded well to abstract conceptual explanations for mathematics might respond much better to concrete worked examples for grammar. The agent needed to develop a model of each student's preferences at the topic level, not just at the student level.

Canvas Gallery: Additional Design Templates

Customer Onboarding Agent Canvas

Goal: guide new customers through product setup and initial value realization, reducing churn from early frustration and increasing time-to-value.

Core agents: onboarding coordinator (manages the onboarding sequence), product guide (answers product questions and helps with setup), progress tracker (monitors completion of key onboarding milestones).

Memory: customer profile and account configuration; progress through onboarding milestones; questions asked and answers given; engagement signals.

Tools: CRM integration, product usage data, knowledge base, ticketing system for issues that need support escalation.

Governance: human escalation for customers who are at risk of churn (defined by specific engagement signals), no autonomous changes to customer account configuration without explicit request, all interactions logged to CRM.

Key questions: What are the critical milestones that predict long-term customer success? How does the onboarding sequence differ by customer segment? What are the signals that indicate a customer needs human intervention rather than automated guidance?

Supply Chain Monitoring Agent Canvas

Goal: detect supply chain disruptions and degradations early enough for operations teams to respond before they impact production.

Core agents: data collector (aggregates information from multiple supply chain data sources), pattern analyzer (detects anomalies and trends), alert generator (produces structured alerts with impact assessment).

Memory: historical supply chain performance baselines; past disruptions and their impact; threshold calibration history; supplier performance profiles.

Tools: supplier portals, shipping tracking APIs, quality system integration, news feed monitoring.

Governance: all alerts reviewed by operations manager before action is taken; false positive tracking for threshold calibration; escalation path for alerts indicating potential production impact.

Key questions: What data sources are available and how reliable are they? What detection thresholds distinguish actionable signals from noise? How are alert thresholds maintained as normal operating ranges change seasonally or as business changes?

Content Moderation Agent Canvas

Goal: review user-generated content accurately and efficiently, removing harmful content while minimizing impact on legitimate content.

Core agents: fast classifier (reactive, handles clear approve and clear reject cases), deliberative reviewer (handles ambiguous cases), escalation coordinator (manages routing to human review).

Memory: policy guidelines with version history; example violations by type; false positive cases for calibration; emerging violation pattern library.

Tools: content analysis APIs, image analysis (if applicable), user history lookup, policy documentation.

Governance: false positive rate monitoring with alert when threshold exceeded; regular audits of automatic decisions; human review queue management; clear appeals process for users whose content was removed.

Key questions: What are the most important policy dimensions to enforce and in what priority order? What are the consequences of different types of errors (false positives vs false negatives)? How does the system handle emerging violation patterns that weren't anticipated at design time?

Educational Personalization Agent Canvas

Goal: adapt the learning experience for each student to maximize engagement and learning outcomes.

Core agents: assessment analyzer (interprets student performance data to understand comprehension and gaps), content selector (chooses appropriate next content based on student model), explanation adapter (adjusts explanation depth and style).

Memory: per-student knowledge map (what has been learned and to what depth); learning pace history; preferences by content type and topic; past engagement patterns.

Tools: learning management system, content library, assessment engine, engagement analytics.

Governance: no changes to formal assessments or grades without instructor review; parent/guardian visibility into adaptation decisions if applicable; regular review of adaptation effectiveness by education team.

Key questions: How is student progress measured in a way that distinguishes genuine understanding from pattern-matching on assessments? How are adaptations adjusted when a student's circumstances change (new school year, subject change)? How is the system designed to support rather than replace teacher judgment?

Insights from Across the Case Studies

Looking across all of these deployments, several patterns emerge that are worth drawing out explicitly.

The importance of failure mode inventory. Before deploying any of these systems, the teams built explicit lists of how the system could fail, what the consequences would be, and how each failure mode would be detected and addressed. This exercise, which took anywhere from a day to a week depending on system complexity, consistently revealed failure modes that weren't visible from the design. Systematic failure mode analysis before deployment is one of the highest-leverage practices I've seen.

The value of conservative initial deployment. In every case, the initial deployment was more conservative than the eventual production configuration: more human review, more conservative thresholds, narrower scope. Expanding from a conservative baseline as confidence builds is much safer and produces better outcomes than trying to get the full design right from the start.

The underrated importance of feedback collection. The systems that improved most over time were those where feedback collection was built in from day one, even before it was clear exactly what would be done with the feedback. Systems where feedback collection was added after deployment often had gaps in what was collected, leading to decisions based on incomplete information.

The role of domain expertise. In every case, the system design benefited substantially from deep involvement of domain experts: HR professionals in the onboarding case, operations managers in the supply chain case, experienced moderators in the content moderation case, educators in the learning case. Domain expertise identified requirements and constraints that weren't visible from the engineering perspective and helped calibrate what "good" looked like for the system's outputs.

www.ingramcontent.com/pod-product-compliance
Lightning Source LLC
LaVergne TN
LVHW052321200926
848481LV00002B/633